FOREWORD BY MARLENA GRAVES

CASEY TYGRETT

THE

PRACTICE

OF

REMEMBERING

UNCOVERING *the*
PLACE *of* MEMORIES *in*
OUR SPIRITUAL LIFE

An imprint of InterVarsity Press
Downers Grove, Illinois

To Holley and the B,

who create memories with light and color every day.

InterVarsity Press
P.O. Box 1400 | Downers Grove, IL 60515-1426
ivpress.com | email@ivpress.com

©2019 by Casey K. Tygrett

All rights reserved. No part of this book may be reproduced in any form without written permission from InterVarsity Press. First published by InterVarsity Press as *As I Recall: Discovering the Place of Memories in Our Spiritual Life*.

InterVarsity Press® is the publishing division of InterVarsity Christian Fellowship/USA®. For more information, visit intervarsity.org.

Scripture quotations, unless otherwise noted, are from the New Revised Standard Version Bible, copyright © 1989 National Council of the Churches of Christ in the United States of America. Used by permission. All rights reserved worldwide.

While any stories in this book are true, some names and identifying information may have been changed to protect the privacy of individuals.

Published in association with the literary agent Don Gates of The Gates Group, www.the-gates-group.com.

The publisher cannot verify the accuracy or functionality of website URLs used in this book beyond the date of publication.

Cover design: David Fassett
Interior design: Daniel van Loon

Images: Colorful abstract background: © Alexandre Bardol / EyEm / Getty Images
        Abstract bubble background: © Sudhir Kumar / EyeEm Premium / Getty Images

ISBN 978-1-5140-0730-3 (print) | ISBN 978-1-5140-0731-0 (digital)

Printed in the United States of America ∞

Library of Congress Cataloging-in-Publication Data
A catalog record for this book is available from the Library of Congress.

30 29 28 27 26 25 24 23 | 8 7 6 5 4 3 2 1

CONTENTS

Foreword by Marlena Graves | 1

Introduction
A Question Before Remembering | 5

1 How We Got Here | 13
Practice: Narrating a Memory | 25

2 The Art of Noticing Shells | 26
Practice: Journaling | 37

3 Living with Shells | 39
Practice: Staging a Memory | 54

4 The Weight of Shells | 56
Pause | 71

5 Every Memory Belongs | 72
Practice: Writing a Spiritual Autobiography | 85

6 Remembering Who We Are | 87
Practice: Finding Sabbath Rest | 106

7 Coming Back Again | 108
Practice: The Examen for Memories | 127

8 I've Felt Like This Before | 128
Practice: Writing Your Own Psalm | 142

9 A Familiar Table | 144
Practice: Opening Your Table | 163

10 Remember, Be Here Now | 165
Pause | 183

11 A Future Memory | 184
Pause | 195

12 A Closing Post-it Note | 196

Acknowledgments | 201

Notes | 203

FOREWORD

Marlena Graves

Casey Tygrett writes, "Without memory, there is no formation, whether those memories are joyful and treasured, ambiguous and circumstantial, or traumatic. We are God's memory-made beings." The first time I read Tygrett's words, I was fascinated. I turned his words around and around in my mind. How revelatory. He's right. The trajectory of my life is based on my experiences, my memory of those experiences, and what God and I do with them. But not only in my life: American culture, the geographical and cultural milieu in which I find myself, is shaped by collective memories—what we choose to remember and what we choose to forget.

Growing up in poverty in the United States has had a profoundly formative effect on my life. It was at a Christian college that I realized how very poor I was, and I resented it. Not so much because I wanted what everyone else had, but because of the many inconveniences and obstacles poverty placed in my way. Most of my classmates did not experience the tremendous stress that I did. I remembered being utterly shocked that in 1996 a chemistry book was $114. That was just one book. And I needed many more for my classes freshman year. How was I supposed to study if I could not even afford my books?

Coupled with my memories of need are memories of God coming through in spectacular ways for me. I was completely dependent on God to provide for everything I needed. He often used the church—people I knew. But God also provided in inexplicable ways, in supernatural ways, in particular-to-me ways that only God could know and bring a about. It is why I am convinced God exists. It is why I am confident God is a good Father despite the presence of evil in the world and my unanswered questions about the problem of evil. God intervened in my poverty-stricken life, where I had no networks or connections. Yes, I resented the material obstacles and suffering poverty presented, but looking back, I can honestly sing along to "Broke" by Lecrae, a rap artist who happens to be a Christian: "Being broke made me rich." I can testify that God does not break a bruised reed and that he listens to the cry of the poor. And not just the financially poor—but to those impoverished in other ways. My life and memories are God-haunted. As Tygrett explains, "We engage our memories in tandem with God because they are the starting points for who we are now and who we have yet to become."

Tygrett does not merely psychologize or spiritualize our memories and their formative aspects. As a good counselor, pastor, spiritual director, and yea even theologian, Tygrett knows that we are not Gnostics. Our memories and the spiritual formation that flows from them affect our whole beings, our bodies. We incarnate our memories and even the trauma of our ancestors. Tygrett points to cutting edge neuroscience and epigenetics to explain how our body recalls generations of trauma (or even joy). To engage our memories in tandem with God, we have to face them; not because we are sadists, but because it's only in facing them and their effects in our lives that they can be "redeemed" (as Tygrett notes) so that we can move forward.

In spiritual formation we might often ask ourselves how we are going to change today or how we might experience God today. However, as Tygrett deftly points out, "We rarely ask, How did I come to the habits and actions I'm taking today?" This is important. Why is it that I struggle in certain situations and not in others? What do God and memory have to do with it? Engage with Tygrett's words and wisdom carefully, and you will discover why it is so important. This book makes a definite contribution to the realm of spiritual formation, and I for one will continue to ponder Tygrett's words and wisdom. You made a good decision to pick up this book. I am happy to recommend it to you. If it has been helpful, let Casey Tygrett know too. I sure will.

INTRODUCTION

A Question Before Remembering

Everything must have a beginning ... and that beginning
must be linked to something that went before.

MARY SHELLEY

A s I recall ...
  We were making the long trek from Rockford, Illinois, to Naperville, Illinois. Perhaps this trip isn't as long as many cross-country journeys, but there are times when a drive through cornfields and into the warehouse-dense Chicago suburbs feels near to eternity.

The acres of corn and soy stretched in either direction. As the expressway wove into the suburbs, with warehouses and manufacturing plants rising over the cropland, we listened to our favorite podcast, *Wait, Wait ... Don't Tell Me.*

My daughter, moving into an age when she was old enough to understand sarcasm, chuckled from the back seat and smoothed the miles that passed underneath us.

Our exit approached, and as we turned from the artery of a Chicago expressway to the veins of the crisscrossing local roads, the podcast hosts talked about a new study that found a certain type of alcohol was excellent in the fight against osteoporosis —*tequila.*

Margarita sales among seniors likely went up exponentially after this study, but that's merely speculation.

We laughed together at the curious story and continued on our journey. Going to visit the grandparents was a regular occurrence, which made it all the more interesting when we took the same trip some weeks later.

The same expressway passed beneath us, and when we took that same exit my daughter said, "Hey, this is where we heard that thing about tequila." I believe the phrase you're looking for right now is "Train up a child in the way he should go . . ." (Prov 22:6 KJV).

From that day on, every time we hit the exit we spoke its new name: *Tequila Road.* I honestly can't recall the *actual* name of that exit. However, the random news report is now part of Tygrett family lore.

Why is that?

TO REMEMBER OR FORGET

Why can I remember the hospital transport person who graciously pushed my wife's wheelchair as we left the hospital when my daughter was born, but for the life of me, I cannot remember his name? While his name might escape me, his gentleness and candor do not.

I do remember he had a stoop in his stature and a quiet smile on his face as he handed us a homemade CD (yes, back in the day) of songs that he thought best celebrated a new life coming into the world. Louis Armstrong's "What a Wonderful World" was the opening track.

That I remember. Sitting at the keyboard right now, however, I couldn't tell you my schedule for tomorrow unless at least one piece of technology in my life decides to *ding*.

Why is that?

Why can my wife remember all the details of our first date but little about our honeymoon?

Why can I remember with clarity the color of the tiles in the church basement where, in three weeks' time one November, we mourned the passing of both my great-uncle and my great-grandfather?

Neuroscientist V. S. Ramachandran says, "How can a three-pound mass of jelly that you can hold in your palm imagine angels, contemplate the meaning of infinity, and even question its own place in the cosmos?"[1]

I would be content most days with remembering my schedule and my Google password.

The real question here is simply, *Why do we remember some things and not others?* Why do we hold memories from nearly thirty-five years ago in the vault, while a conversation from thirty-five minutes ago might slip into oblivion?

Is it more than just brain function? Is there something deeper fastening those moments into my mind? What is the purpose of what we *do* remember?

A step further and we ask this question: Does God find anything of value, anything helpful and constructive, in our lives of archived memories? Does he work with both what we retain and what we fail to remember? Memories come to us all the time:

sitting in traffic, when we take in a certain smell, or when we watch something happen that we are certain has happened before. Déjà vu, they call it, or the "black cat" in *The Matrix*.[2]

What role do these slippery scenes have in the very real and deep work of living eternally with Jesus starting here and now? Do they contribute anything to the way of savoring life that Jesus gives "abundantly"? (Jn 10:10)

THE TOPIC AT HAND

The question of memory—specifically what memories mean in light of our life of faith—has always been with me. I suppose memory and memories have been the subtext for all pastoral work I have done in the last twenty-two years.

Helping people remember the story of the gospel, to remember times when they were close to God, and to bring to mind memories of life and hope that keep them going— these are all part and parcel of walking with others, walking with Jesus.

It hasn't escaped me, however, that even with this powerful subtext we are tempted to say, "The past is behind us. It doesn't matter. It's irrelevant." Perhaps I would have agreed with these statements before, but today I believe that memories (and memory) *matter*. Even though transformation is seen as a future-oriented work, memory matters in the sacred work of spiritual transformation.

So why bother with a conversation about memory, and again does God have anything to do with our recall?

This is the critical question that sets into motion the conversation that we have in front of us. It is a conversation with God, in God's presence, and one that is important to our spiritual growth and transformation.

My hope is to invite you to this conversation in all the many and varied ways that it is present in our comings and goings through life with Jesus. In this book you will encounter reflections on memory as it comes to light in large sections of the Bible. At the end of each chapter you will find either a "Practice" or a "Pause." Since spiritual formation is about both *being* and *doing*, it makes sense to have both work and rest included. You are welcome to do both.

I encourage you to spend time with each practice or pause and allow the content of the chapter to draw you to prayer, silence, or action based on what you have heard. The practices may take some time, so give yourself space to come back to each practice or pause when you have time.

Now, as in most cases, the best place to start is on a beach.

WE ALL GATHER SHELLS

One of my favorite places in the world is Grand Cayman, one of the beautiful Cayman Islands in the middle of the Caribbean. For what it's worth, the times we have gone to Grand Cayman as a family have been at the tail end of tropical storm season. While we risked our lives for the beauty, it was also 75 percent off the peak season cost.

The risk is well worth it.

We have pictures of my daughter walking the beach at various heights and life stages, leaving progressively larger footprints in the sand. We spent many evenings watching for the "green flash"—a serendipitous moment where the sunset meets the

horizon and a brief, brilliant flash of green light hits the sky. We
never captured the green flash, but we never ceased to search for
it either.

As we walked the beach at night with our skin and spirits tired
from the hot days near the equator, we would search for shells.
Some of those shells sit in a glass jar not far from where I'm
writing—they have accompanied us through two moves, not to
mention surviving the plane ride back to the States.

They are gentle signs of our presence in a place and time in the
past. We saw them, felt them, placed them in a cup and valued
them enough to pack them wrapped in our underwear so they
would survive the flight unharmed.

The shells are an apt image for our memories. We walk through
life encountering God, gore, and grace, and we collect those *experiences* along the way. We then weed through the shells, keeping
some and letting others topple into the surf, and those we keep
become a fixed item from a moment in time—a *memory*.

The memories build, and we are able to bring the jar out and
show them to friends and family and tell the *story* this collection
of memories carries. My daughter has grown up gathering shells,
and she has learned the *script* for how we conduct ourselves on
the beach at night. Perhaps one day she'll take her kids to the
salt-washed shores as well.

The imagery of gathering shells helps me understand both
how we come to have and hold our memories, and what critical
significance they hold for our formation with Jesus. The
framework of *experiences, memories, stories,* and *scripts* is one that
we will return to throughout the book. It will serve as a foundation for us as we examine not only how memory affects us but

also how the Scriptures and the Spirit guide us in being formed through the content of our memories.

Perhaps as we begin, the best thing you can do is to imagine your memories as gathered shells, textured and colorful, laid out in front of you. As you look at them, ask yourself these two simple questions: What do I recall? Why?

Bring out your shells. We now begin to remember.

1

HOW WE GOT HERE

How we perceive the world and how we act in it are products of how and what we remember. We're all just a bundle of habits shaped by our memories.

JOSHUA FOER

I woke up this morning and made my usual half-hearted slap at the table beside the bed. The slap, intended to shut off my alarm, happens every morning. Even though my unconscious aim should be far better than it is, I never seem to turn it off on the first attempt. Through many trials, I finally switched it off.

I slid sideways out of bed, my feet touched the floor, and I began the journey to find some clothes. At that point, I hadn't actively given thought to what I was doing. I don't have to think through how to stand up; I don't have to analyze the steps toward swinging my arm at the bedside table. These are embedded deep in what is called my nondeclarative memory, the memory we use for well-worn habits and rituals that require little to no conscious thought.[1] This memory seeps into my limbs, causing my body to operate more or less independently.

Now, trying to find my clothes is a different story. I'm reaching back to eight or nine hours ago when I took those clothes off and laid them, well, where did I lay them? Oh yes, on the chair. I knew that. There they are.

What emerges in this illustration is that there are several stories at work in my common movements. The story comes to mind, for instance, of why we bought the chair in the corner of our bedroom. Which of course is tied to the story of how we decided to buy the house with the bedroom that required the chair in the corner, a story that lives just around the corner from why we bought a house in the town we currently live in. From there, we see quite clearly the story of why we left the town we lived in before.

I also carry deeper whispers: experiences, events, happenings, messages repeated to me throughout childhood, the bigger designs and desires of my life, and the bigger dramas of my relationships and inner world. I carry memories of being loved or being ignored, being encouraged or discouraged.

They all come with me. They are my—*our*—companions, our friends.

This is the stuff of our every day. We all wake up in the morning, and we *walk*. We do things. We make things. We remember to pick up dry cleaning, remember the shortcut to work if traffic is bad, and remember our child's favorite color or sandwich or shirt. We slap the alarm and search for our pants in the dark. We have daily memories that shape everything that we do.

But why do we do *what* we do—in the way that we do it? Why don't we do otherwise?

MEMORY-MADE PEOPLE

Pioneering neuroscientist Eric Kandel says,

> Without the binding force of memory, experience would be splintered into as many fragments as there are moments

in life. Without the mental time travel provided by memory, we would have no awareness of our personal history, no way of remembering the joys that serve as the luminous milestones of our life. We are who we are because of what we learn and what we remember.[2]

When it comes to our engagement with God and our formation around the life and teachings of Jesus, these memories come with us; they help make us, so to speak. We are at work in the renewal, care, and growth of our souls, and as Dallas Willard says, our soul is "that aspect of your whole being that correlates, integrates, and enlivens everything going on in the various dimensions of the self."[3]

> *Without memory, there is no formation, whether those memories are joyful and treasured, ambiguous and circumstantial, or traumatic. We are God's memory-made beings.*

In other words, everything that is true of us has been etched into our souls from our memories of life with God, self, and others. We lose our selves when we lose our memories, and without our memories, growth and formation simply wander into oblivion.

In fact, every person alive today is living a certain way because of their memories and the stories that result. Throbbing beneath the surface of thoughts, words, attitudes, and perspectives are dramas built on ground that ran beneath their feet long ago.

Without memory, there is no formation, whether those memories are joyful and treasured, ambiguous and circumstantial, or traumatic. We are God's memory-made beings.

Of course, the "memory" that connects most deeply to our formation isn't whether or not we can remember our online passwords (it may be time to change all of my passwords to "Forgot My Password") or our grocery list.

Instead, the kind of memory we're talking about is the embedded recall of lived experiences, the experiences that make us who we are and give our spiritual lives the raw material for transformation through God's Spirit. So, what do we do with that rough, unkneaded clay?

It is here we find the gift of engaging our memories: *we engage our memories in tandem with God because they are the starting points for who we are now and who we have yet to become.* This is the most compelling call we have for a work that will, at times, feel beyond the scope of our abilities. However, we have no choice—whatever we do today or tomorrow will flow out of the memories that live deep within us.

Some of our memories are broken and misguided and need to be redeemed. Some of our memories are beautiful and can give us energy for present challenges. Some of our memories are signs of a person we used to be and can give us perspective and wisdom on where we are and where we are headed in our life with Jesus. And we are not alone:

For Esther, "such a time as this" required that she remember the times prior to the present moment.

For Moses, the phrase "the God of Abraham, Isaac, and Jacob" required that he remember campfires and the stories he heard of an ancient promise now held in the present.

For us, we may hear Jesus say, "So if the Son sets you free, you will be free indeed" (Jn 8:36 NIV), and we are immediately taken back to memories of slavery and oppression so we might savor the honey-thick goodness of today's redemption.

Without these memories, we cannot *become*. Without these memories, the narrative of our lives begins to disintegrate and lose its way.

A NOTE ABOUT MEMORIES

Before we can go further, it is important to name a reality that many of us face when it comes to memories. Namely, the things we remember aren't always cute anecdotes or charming, CD-dispensing hospital employees.

Our memories can be dark specters, unkind and unyielding.

They can be monsters of the grandest design.

Many of us have experienced physical or emotional abuse, failure of jobs or relationships, and failures of nerve throughout our histories. Revisiting those memories sounds like self-inflicted torture, and that reality requires respect and tenderness.

Allowing the Spirit of Jesus to redeem and renew past pain for the sake of our formation is not perfect or painless in and of itself. Any process of change requires a form of dying, of letting go of structures and conceptions that hold us in the place of suffering or stagnancy.

As Jesus says, "Very truly, I tell you, unless a grain of wheat falls into the earth and dies, it remains just a single grain; but if it dies, it bears much fruit" (Jn 12:24).

Even allowing God's gentle and tender presence to move through us as we draw our memories close feels like embracing a flame, and we can't ignore the possibilities of further wounds.

Yet we may also see a redeemed, uncontainable harvest from digging deep and bringing out those seeds planted within us. Such is the good and terrifying mystery of formation.

In the pain of our memories, it is important to call to mind the image of Jesus from Matthew: "He will not break a bruised reed or quench a smoldering wick" (Mt 12:20).

His presence is sweet, strong, and easy—tending to us like a delicate plant swayed by winds no firmer than a child's breath. We need that presence in us as we journey with our memories; they can be places where the darkest corners are darker still, places where we are already wounded and another blow could be fatal. Though it is not always the memory that wounds.

Our memories can be dark specters, unkind and unyielding. They can be monsters of the grandest design.

The reality may also be that the memories are the beauty and the *present* is actually painful. Perhaps we have photographs hanging on the wall of a time we loved, and we are reticent to replace them with more recent photos because things are not as we believe they should be. Instead of avoiding and fearing our *memories*, we cling to them because our present darkness is too great.

In a strange twist, we cling to memories of the past because the present is too brutal and the future too uncertain. Yet our movement toward our memories in partnership with God renews the present because we are offered the wise and imaginative view of our Creator. We need the savory scent of why that past was beautiful to remind us of what is present in front of us here and now.

It is helpful to move through these memories and the reflections that will come with a spiritual director or counselor. Choosing someone who is compassionate, who knows our story and is willing to sit with us in the midst of what we're reading and processing is helpful. My recommendation is that if this book becomes too difficult, please move from reading to conversation with someone who can walk with you through the difficulties.

WE REMEMBER WITH

I have memories of events that I was not even alive to experience. Somewhere in my mom's house is a book of photos, born of Polaroids and Kodak film painstakingly developed to find both the smiles of children and finger-blurred shots that could be *anything*. I have memories of looking at pictures while my parents or grandparents explain what's happening, why those clothes were actually in style, and why certain people look irritated in every single shot.

These are not my memories, at least not initially. Once explained, however, I realize my place in the narrative—where my picture fits—and they become sacred texts of my family and world.

Every sacred text, even the Bible, has a memory of sorts; it has a history, a "that which came before." The Bible itself is so full of memories that the most dangerous way to read it is to pretend that each verse dropped out of the sky completely devoid of history.

It would be like looking at my childhood photographs and pretending they had taken place only the day before. Each woven phase of the Bible comes from stories passed around campfires, family tables, and gathered communities. It is a book of memories.

Every word of Paul or Moses or John (pick your favorite) rises from their own living memoir, just as ours do. They speak out of the memory-laden context of life with God in their own place, time, and situation. They are not our memories from experience, but we integrate them into our stories just the same.

More than that, every illustration and teaching that we hear in our churches and fellowships is full of memories—stories heard, classes taken, experiences endured. Think about the first time we heard the name *God*. Who was it that taught us? Where were we when we heard that teaching? How has that teaching impacted our life up to this point? How has it formed us? Without engaging who we have been taught God *is*, we will remain in the dark about our present challenges and future implications.

We have been given a lens for seeing God, and that lens will form the way we see the world. The least we can do is learn the particulars of how that lens affects us. This is the critical value of our memories in our formation.

As Joyce Rupp notes, "Our understanding and our experience of God shapes our image of God and our spirituality."[4]

And we never remember alone. We are always sharing memories and the lessons therein with a bigger group: a family, a church, or a Christian tradition that spans millennia.

All of these things make it impossible to assume that somehow today is immune to the past and the future is exempt from today. All memories matter, and our present-day journey with Jesus is reflective of everything that has gone before.

Any transformation that happens in us through the beautiful Spirit of Jesus leaps from the shoulders of those who have helped fill our memories with the stories of ourselves and our God.

For you, is there a memory that has risen to the surface as you read? Something that causes you to shiver because you're unsure of the vulnerability it creates?

Is there a moment in your past—dark and dangerous or fluorescent and hopeful—that shapes and frames you today?

Where did it begin? Who gave it to you? Where does Jesus' call to transformation lead you from here? Keep these questions in mind as they may be helpful for a practice at the end of the chapter.

MOVING TOWARD OUR MEMORIES

To put it in terms of a definition, spiritual formation is learning to live like Jesus within the skin we're in. We are compelled then to come to terms with what that skin looks like, which means we have to reengage the experiences and memories that have tinted and weathered the skin we're in.

Our engagement with our own memories also trains us for peaceful, civil interactions with others. When we see people acting in ways we consider outrageous or irrational, we might do well to remember that everyone we encounter is the way they are because of their memories. Of course, understanding this does not inspire us to enable but instead to empathize.

We are all containers of shells, some rough and broken and some colorful and fully formed. To count these shells is to know who we are, and to know who we are is to experience the wildness of redemption, mystery, and conviction that come through being "searched" and "known" (Ps 139) by a careful and loving God.

How do we go about engaging with our memories in an honest and transformational way?

Throughout the conversation, we must continue to come back to our key memories. We do this in order for the Spirit of God to help us make sense of and even redeem some of the shells we have collected over the years. The four movements that follow give us footing for engaging with the shells that may rise to the surface. Feel free to come back to these movements as you enter into the broader discussion about memories.

First, we bring the shell. This may be a difficult movement as our memories contain painful thoughts and harmful narratives that many of us have worked hard to release and redeem. You can practice "bringing your shells" in personal practice as you read or as you are accompanied by a therapist, counselor, or spiritual director you trust.

Second, we honestly engage with the implications. As someone who has spent the last twenty years teaching in public settings, I have had my share of follow-up correspondence regarding messages and teachings I've given. I have in my personal files some encouraging notes—people finding hope, challenge, encouragement, or enlightenment—and I turn to those when days become difficult.

However, I have one memory—a shell—that comes up as soon as I think about feedback. After one particular message regarding the intersection of science and the Bible, I heard (secondhand by the way, thus increasing the bitterness) that one of our staff received an email saying, "The Bible needs a better interpreter than Casey."

I have carried that memory forward since 2011.

It has *formed* me.

So what are the implications of this memory for my formation in Christ? What does this nugget have to do with the way I see my calling, vocation, identity—even my self-confidence in presenting what I've been asked to present?

We bring the memories, stories, and scripts to the front, and we engage with the question, What did that moment, that experience, that emotion mean then?

Third, we begin to look at what those implications have created. The experiences and memories we've gathered have created some sort of story. Stories about God, ourselves, and others are woven out of what we have experienced. The implications of my credibility and fitness to teach being questioned shapes my pride, the depth of my preparation, and cultivates in me the ability to realize not everyone is my biggest fan.

As we look at the implications of our memories of failure and success, frustration and fruitfulness, mystery and misunderstanding, we begin to see that these memories have shaped us immensely. We have something within us that directly ties to these memories and stories. That "something" is raw material for the journey of formation through redemption that causes the Spirit of God to salivate.

Finally, we explore how the Spirit of God is wooing and moving us through these particular memories and stories. Drawing on the experiences we've identified and the memories and stories they have written, we have an opportunity to revisit the daily scripts through which we've been living up to this point. We come to a sense of *why*—even if it is only a flicker—we are who we are, and we begin to ask questions about where God may be leading us as a result.

Are there conversations we need to have in order to re-engage long-accepted narratives that came as a result of our memories of a mom, dad, brother, sister or significant other? Are there practices such as prayer, fasting, and sabbath that we need to engage in so that we can begin to redeem narratives of foolishness, compulsion, and slavery? Is God moving in us so that we may have space to consider our past as *relevant* to our present and therefore understand the intense need for healing that has always been within us?

As we go, we bring these four movements into our observation and dialogue with the stories of Scripture. In them we find that the complicated litany of our memories is both messy and miraculous. In so seeing, we can take a deep breath in our own formation and release the pressures of perfection. Instead, we lean into the grace of the good journey.

PRACTICE

We opened the discussion of how important our memories are for creating the selves we bring into the journey of transformation with Jesus. During the reading, it is likely that a memory came to the surface for you. It may have been a painful memory or simply a regret you had put well behind you.

You may have had several memories come to the surface, but at this point it is important to identify one that you'd like to work with.

In this practice, the point is to establish a "text" for that memory that you can return to throughout the rest of the book. Find a journal and use the following writing prompt to sketch out one particularly important memory that has come to the surface during your reading. A writing prompt is simply a question or phrase to get things started, and in this case it gives you a place to begin your memory sketch.

Make sure to provide as much detail as possible: from smells, sights, sounds of the memory in question to the backstory or context of the event. Write from your perspective, even though your perspective is limited, but leave room to bring in details from the perspective of others involved in the situation. Try to explore as many different angles on the memory as possible so you have a large and clear picture to work with. Keep this memory "text" with you as you read the rest of the book.

Prompt: I remember the moment when . . .

2

THE ART OF
NOTICING SHELLS

*We are not mere spectators or performers; rather we
are active participants in God's world.*

Susan Phillips

Writing a book requires gallons of hot tea. At least that has been my experience thus far. Many times, the waiting period for the kettle to boil is simply a good reason to postpone returning to the blinking cursor. As I was writing this chapter, I took such a detour and delighted in the fact that we had a brand-new container of honey. Peeling off the safety seal, I did what every wise adult does—I licked off the excess.

Suddenly, I was mentally transported back to the McDonald's in the town where I grew up. I remembered dipping chicken nuggets in a small container of honey. That golden-sweet burst of honey sent me backward nearly thirty years in a matter of seconds.

Apparently, the experience is still alive somewhere in my head.

I noticed it, and it led me on the mental time travel back to my childhood. It all started with a taste, a sensory experience.

A SENSE OF THINGS

Before we truly remember anything, it starts as an experience. It is a moment when our senses (sight, sound, taste, smell, and touch) interact with the world around us. Those signals are then shuffled into our short-term memory.

Our short-term memory is delicate. When the senses feed data to the brain, it goes to a holding area in the prefrontal cortex called short-term or working memory. In this waiting room, information will live for about thirty seconds before it is either whisked away toward the hippocampus, which facilitates the journey to long-term memory, or dropped into the abyss as new shells are collected moment by moment.[1] Remembering *anything* is a delicate affair.

However, there is an exception for shells that come from our sense of smell. Smells proceed directly to our limbic system where they are immediately taken in without translation. There is virtually no short-term memory with odors. It is all long term.[2]

The reason for this is that the area of the brain that processes smell is located close to the hippocampus where memories often find their home in our brains.[3] *All* smell goes to long-term memory.

So here's to you, skunks and rotten milk. We will never forget you.

From the perspective of Scripture this is interesting, given scenes like Peter's encounter with Jesus on the beach, where John mentions that they were near a "charcoal fire" (Jn 21:9). The only other place in the New Testament we find the same Greek word for "charcoal fire" (*anthrakia*) also involves Peter. The first of Peter's charcoal fires is when he betrays Jesus (Jn 18:18).

I wonder, could it be that the smell experience of one fire was redeemed and set free by the matching scent of the other? What could we learn about the way God interacts with our own smells, tastes, sights, and sounds?

Before we truly remember anything, it starts as an experience. All formation begins with these experiences: sights, sounds, tastes, and smells.

The experience of the fire, or perhaps the sense memory we carry of failure and success and everything in between, sinks in and stays. It can be recalled easily. The smell memory of one fire condemns and pains Peter, but the smell memory of a second both redeems the first and forms something in him for the future.

These little experiences—the smells of food or a familiar fragrance, the sight of someone we find beautiful, or the sound of music that stirs us—begin the journey into our God-designed selves. Therefore, all formation begins with these experiences: sight, sound, taste, smell, and touch.

We walk through life and gather experiences—shells if you will—like these. In this way we have a common bond with the people of Scripture. Every character in the Bible had a sensory life, gathering shells through their biological receptors and trying to make sense of them.

When we read the Scriptures we are reading accounts of people who are *experiencing* things for the first time, returning to an experience long past, or being reminded of something beautiful or brutal that shaped them indefinitely.

We—and all those who have come before us—pick up the same experience, and we *sense* it: we feel its edges, notice its color, smell the distinctive character (for shells it is the sickly seafood salt smell) of the experience, and we try to make sense of what it is.

Is it beautiful?

How would we describe the color—the tones, the shades, wrapped around the ridges and swirls?

Has it been damaged?

Does the hard edge scrape our hand, leaving a blemish or a mark?

Is it at all strange then that when the command to "do this in remembrance of me" (Lk 22:19) falls on the ears of Jesus' disciples, it is followed by a *sensory* experience—a meal? Not only that but a sensory experience rooted in a larger *remembered* story called Passover?

MEMORIES ARE BORN FROM EXPERIENCES

My daughter and I were talking and I asked her, "What is your earliest memory?"

I asked this question on a chilly and wet fall day, her head nearly submerged in a bowl of cereal. She looked up puzzled, so I clarified. "Okay, so you don't remember being born right? What's your next memory?"

She paused, swallowed, and said, "I remember preschool."

It makes sense. Researchers say we don't begin to truly collect memories until we're around three years old. While that seems like an arbitrary age, there is a reason why that age matters.

Around three, children begin to understand and retain sensory details about the world they are involved in.[4] They ask questions. They begin to draw in values and experiences. Elements are falling into place in their little minds—stories are emerging that

will help them make sense of the world, memories that will help
define the contours of the world they live in.

In Petina Gappah's novel *The Book of Memory*, an albino
woman (aptly named Memory) from Zimbabwe retells the
story of the murder for which she is imprisoned. Memory says,
"Until you attempt to write the story of your life, you cannot
quite understand just how hard it is to grasp at the beginning."
The beginning is the moment our prefrontal cortex begins to
develop, and we are able to summon the words to make sense of
our experiences.[5]

The transition from experience to remembering entails being
able to make sense of our experiences. Here is where things
become problematic. The move from experience to memory is
called *encoding*, and everything from emotions to physical limitations can affect that process.[6]

David Eagleman goes so far as to say, "We are astoundingly
poor observers. . . . We believe we're seeing the world just fine
until it's called to our attention that we're not."[7]

Clearly, experiences are sketchy. On the one hand, they are
highly dependent on our own perspective, place, and time even
though they are shared by every human being on the planet. The
use of senses is *universal*.

However, the gathering of experiences is also *unique*. I cannot
experience the sight, sound, and stimulation of a film from any
other perspective than as a white male living in the Midwest. I
can engage with the experiences of others who share my universal way of sensing, but they have a unique set of filters through
which they gather experiences that distinguishes their shells
from my own.

James Elkins talks about how even the sense of sight is more complicated than we might believe: "Our eyes are not ours to command; they roam where they will and then tell us they have only been where we have sent them. No matter how hard we look, we see very little of what we look at. . . . Ultimately, seeing alters the thing that is seen and transforms the seer. Seeing is metamorphosis, not mechanism."[8]

These shells so strangely gathered through our senses, these experiences we have gathered become our memories. They attach deeply into our brains (though what part of the brain is still a question for neurologists and neuroscientists).

What we do know is that sensory experiences that become memories move along a complex highway of neurons in our brains, leaping gaps between synapses through chemical or electrical impulses. There are nearly 100 billion neurons in our brains, each making between 5,000 to 10,000 of these connections with other neurons. These biological, electrical kisses are sparked by the stimuli of our experiences and end up painting the landscape of our memories.[9]

The efficient movement of our experiences through this labyrinth of electrified tissue has a lot to do with repetition and significance, especially in terms of detail. The more frequently and attentively information is run down the neurological highway, the better chance those specific details have of moving from the short-term to long-term storage centers.

We actually have three different types of long-term memory: semantic, procedural, and episodic. The semantic is the stored memory of facts and figures without context or details. Procedural memory is the recall of how to do something, tying your shoes, for example. Episodic memory is the mental inscription of events, places, details, and locations.[10] Why is this important?

Imagine this: We feel violated, defeated, and demeaned by someone we love. The facts of our experience (who, what, when, where, and why) are semantic memories attached to the reality of that experience (the impact and the feeling), which fits the episodic category.

These elements then dig deep into our souls. In another example, we experience God as present or as absent, and that idea or fact combines with the emotion of the moment in which this experience lives and grows. It becomes part of how we live, sometimes reflexively, which is procedural memory.

This is why the nourishing part of Bible memorization comes when we move from memorizing Scriptures (note the s) to memorizing Scripture—meaning moving from one or two lines of the Bible to memorizing large stories and themes. Glenn Paauw draws the distinction between these two approaches, calling the former "Bible snacking" and the latter "Bible feasting."[11]

When it comes to our memories, we're more likely to remember the lines of Scripture (semantic memory) if we know the context and circumstances of the audience (episodic memory), and therefore have a better shot at integrating the Scripture naturally into our lives (procedural memory).

SHAPING THE BRAIN

Those experiences that move to long-term memory actually change the physical shape of our brain, cutting a groove through our neurons that other information can pass through or through which we can recall those same moments over and over again.

In her book *The Plastic Mind*, Sharon Begley puts into concrete terms something called *neuroplasticity*, or the ability of our brains to change as a result of the experiences we have and of the environment we are in:

> New synapses, connections between one neuron and another, are the physical manifestations of memories. . . . The brain remakes itself throughout life, in response to outside stimuli to its environment and to experience.[12]

In fact, there is strong evidence that in the act of reading this book your actual brain structure will change based on the experiences and memories you have while reading. As an author, I am literally messing with your mind.

Or we sense the presence of God during a long walk in a forest preserve, and we couch that experience in a season of spiritual or personal struggle. From that moment on, we can go back and retrieve that feeling of God's presence at will because of an alteration in the shape of our brains.

The life of walking with Jesus is connected to these deep and significant memories. The memories that have carved a path in our brains carve a path in our souls as well. Especially when it comes to how we know the ideas behind our faith.

There is a shape to the neural pathways of my brain that caused me to fear thunderstorms as the "coming judgment" in the early stages of my faith. Every lightning strike was a call to repentance. My experiences in the deep red–carpeted church sanctuary where I grew up has cut a path in my brain, and my natural response to the words of God's vengeance and wrath travel down that pathway.

When the paths are healthy, obviously they are beautiful and near-poetic to our spiritual lives. When the paths are misguided, something begins to take shape in us that we don't quite understand but is difficult to avoid in our journey of formation.

Our memories and experiences are clay, stone, and oil pastels that the Spirit of God longs to shape within us as something beautiful.

Of course, these brain-shaping moments are the stuff of spiritual formation as well. If neuroplasticity is possible, then the good news of living in the reality of Jesus and the kingdom of God invites us to believe in *pneumaplasticity,* or the malleability of the spirit.[13]

Our memories and experiences are clay, stone, and oil pastels that the Spirit of God longs to shape within us as something beautiful.

The practice of remembering, of bringing our experiences and memories before God, is an act of *pneumaplasticity*—it shapes the will, drives, and desires that define our lives into that which reflects the radical beauty of God alive in us.

SENSES ALIVE AT NOTRE DAME

In 2012 I had the privilege of going to Paris, France. My wife and daughter and I went in November, and we stayed in a small apartment in the Latin Quarter just above a very "American" restaurant. The building smelled damp and musty from the fall rain as we climbed the spiral staircase up to the fourth floor with our suitcases. There was an elevator, but given its size I would have had to make three *solo* trips, since only one person and one suitcase would fit at a time.

We spent the week walking the streets of Paris. With a five-year-old in tow, our pace was slower and our access points to museums and historical places were limited. The one place where we found ourselves lingering, gazing up and around in awe, was the Notre-Dame de Paris, the legendary cathedral on the banks of the Seine River.

The giant spires were visible from our apartment, which was a beautiful sight to wake up to, but once inside the building we began to understand the reason this space remained legendary. The arching ceiling, hundreds of feet above the cathedral floor, and the ornate sculptures of the twelve disciples above the front entry gave us the sense that by being near the cathedral we were giving ourselves over to something immense.

I imagined all the Parisians—or visitors—who had walked through that place before me. Victor Hugo, novelist and author of *Les Misérables*, no doubt strolled down the side corridors. Perhaps even Ernest Hemingway and F. Scott Fitzgerald made an appearance, altered of mind from a night of revelry and creativity. Perhaps their footsteps matched mine as I paced under the soft lights of the cathedral.

We shook off the soggy November day and found a seat near the middle of the cathedral as a children's choir began to sing. Their voices seemed to rise indefinitely, eternally, and even my daughter sat with rapt attention as their seamless verses flowed one into another. She was as engaged as she could be, not knowing French and being a novice at high liturgy. The priest began the liturgical order, in French of course, and we let the rhythm of his words fill our ears.

We were standing in something with a history, with a memory. We were gathering our own shells as well.

I remember this experience so clearly, and I imagine those who came before did as well. It has *shaped* me—not only my brain but my spirit.

The power of that liturgy, the power of connecting with a tradition of engaging with God that spans centuries, engages our memories for God. In France, they often measure their memories in thousands of years as opposed to the United States where we count in hundreds, but we took part in something that had been happening year after year well before we were even a vapor in this sphere.

In a country often defined as post-Christian, where I was completely unable to decipher the soft French spoken throughout the service, I felt the spirit of Jesus within me leaping with joy. Jesus is found where he is not expected, yet again.

In my experiences. In my memories.

PRACTICE

The practice of journaling aids our cultivation of experiences. It operates as a sort of external hard drive, written in digital or literal ink, serving to hold our experiences for rumination and reflection. Much of my growth and formation have come from writing down experiences— recording the shells, so to speak, like a researcher of my own life—and returning to reread them from time to time. It is difficult to be objective when we experience betrayal, disappointment, and discouragement, yet the opportunity to read it later creates a fresh and new conversation with God on "What in the world was that *actually* about?"

At this point in your reading, consider keeping a journal for your journey through this book. The practice or pause at the end of each chapter is an opportunity for you to reflect in the pages of a journal. Here are some thoughts on beginning a journaling practice.

- Let this be a practice that enlivens you—if you find yourself writing because you *have to* or you *should*, consider putting the journal down. Writing every day may not be a life-giving practice for you. Writing two to three times per week is a healthy rhythm to begin with.

- Decide at the beginning of your journaling practice whether you would want to share what you write with someone, perhaps your spouse, friend, or a spiritual director. You will write differently based on who you believe will read the pages.

- Consider journaling through a single memory in a sitting. Using the four movements listed in the first chapter (see "Moving Toward Our Memories"), bring the memory forward and write about its implications for your life in the present.

- Make time to review your journal frequently. Looking back on past entries can help you to remember the trajectory of your growing intimacy with God.

- It is helpful to write prayers as well. These prayers can reveal what is truly deep within us, and they can also serve as liturgy for our life as we return to them in the future. When we pray these prayers written at different times in our lives, we are taken back to that time, and we can see where God has done the work of redemption in our memories.

3

LIVING WITH SHELLS

Memory is our bridge to the world outside ourselves, to ourselves, and to God.

PAULA FREDRIKSEN

*I*n 1999, I met the woman who would become my wife. Neither Holley nor I had any clue at the time what would happen over the next year, but during a college class trip to Washington, DC, we found time to talk and apparently I was quite persuasive and attractive.

Actually, I was a bit of a mess at that time. Reeling from the ending of another long-term relationship, processing my parents' divorce, and coming to grasp what the pieces of my soul meant for my vocation moving forward, I wasn't at the top of my game.

I was indeed limping.

Yet I remember Holley's attentiveness as if she saw the great loping animal I was at the time and felt compassion for me.

The moment that stands out to me most from that trip was during a silent retreat in the woods just outside of Bethesda, Maryland. We left a challenging few days of studying life in the inner-city neighborhoods of DC to find God in the quiet among the dead January leaves.

In the deep chill of an afternoon walk, free to take time and simply be with God, I sat down at a table and started journaling. My relational world was a mess. I had no concept or compulsion toward how to have a healthy relationship, specifically with the opposite sex.

My life in college was incredibly self-absorbed, ironic given that I was studying to go into pastoral ministry. I thought more of my own needs than others' and struggled to understand the impact of that selfishness on both my male friends in the dorms and the dating relationships I had engaged in since high school.

I put pen to paper under that quiet January gray sky, writing openly to God about this new person I had met. Holley was (and still is) a well of kind strength. Her determination and decisiveness were sweetened by her attention and thoughtfulness, and even though we had been talking only for a few days, I was intrigued.

Yet I had these memories. The experience of being in a relationship but wanting out, unable to end the connection because *What would people think of me?* and *I don't want to hurt her feelings,* which only became a larger memory of hurt and betrayal. The experience of choosing what I wanted, thoughtlessly and in the whim of a moment, led to a memory of watching those I love bending over backward to extend excessive amounts of grace that I took as expected rather than as a gift.

I wrote about Holley in my journal—"Could this be something, someone, that you have in mind for me?"—and I gave full reign to my belief at the time that the will of God was very limited, determinant, and easy to miss. I am paraphrasing from an incomplete memory here, but I believe my next sentence was, "If she is, would you show me?"

I lifted my head. The air cleared in a way that only January air can, and through the bare poplars I saw her. Holley had found me in that low place in the woods, telling me later that she had followed a deer at a distance and happened to find me in the meantime.

This memory—the colors and the cold, the surprise and the soul-searching—comes back to me quite easily. The reason why is that it is part of who I am now. It is part of my memory-shaped world with God.

While you may question the theological or coincidental nature of that moment, while the divinity and serendipity of the scene may seem far-fetched, I cannot deny that it happened. It is a part of me. It is a part of Holley's and my relational world. It is our *story*, despite the fact that we both have very different memories of that same moment.

The woods of Maryland have shaped the *me* of the last eighteen years, and I still remember that day with what feels like photographic clarity.

Spiritual formation always entails movement in our lives—from weakness to strength, from foolishness to wisdom, even paradoxically from the light to the dark when necessary—from "one degree of glory to another" (2 Cor 3:18). How then do the experiences and memories we have gathered become part of our walking with Jesus in the waking world?

MEMORIES BUILD STORIES

We gather the shells of our experiences over time, and as these memories come together en masse they create our *stories*. People come to our home and see our glass jar filled with sand and shells and inevitably ask where they came from. There is a story connected to our little jar of memories, a story of family and life together. It is a story of sunburns, salty eyes, snorkeling, and savage rainstorms. While this seems a bit strong, we live differently because of the story these shells bear witness to.

The story of the most beautiful water we have ever seen.

The story of clean, soft sand.

The story of a family for whom every other beach experience is completely spoiled.

Stories are the underlying structures by which we live; they are the formal and informal narratives we use to make sense of the world. I live by a story that is highlighted by the memories of West Virginia Nazarene churches; life as a high school athlete; being an older brother to a younger sister; moving away from home, much to the pain of my family, and taking up residence in Illinois.

My story is one of learning to love reading later in my college years and being transformed by mystics and monastics at a critical point in my journey. Henri Nouwen and Thomas Merton found me in a moment when I felt so indoctrinated and bound up by the denomination I served that I was ready to leave it all behind.

Graciously, in the past few years I have found beauty in that denomination and in my time there, but at a pregnant moment in my journey with Jesus I found writers who expressed a deeper longing for Jesus that my past experience could not provide.

No doubt you have been mining your memories, examining your collection of shells—what story do you see emerging? Can you see the impact of that story on the decisions you've made today, this week, or even in this moment?

BEING STORYTELLERS

As I noted earlier, children around the age of three develop the mechanism to make sense of experiences and store them as memories. This development helps them to not only make sense of the world but also begin to tell coherent stories of their world. As Lee Eisenberg says, "From [age three] on out, stories will not only entertain you, they will explain you to others and to yourself."[1]

Children are beginning to piece together a life, a reality, an understanding of the world and how they exist within their family, community, and body.

They are creating the story for their lives from the scaffolding of their memories. Stories are the stage on which our journey of formation performs.

We never really stop, either. We simply add layers, complexity, and depth. We forget many things, certainly, but much of our life sticks to us and creates the story we live in this world. Memories create the life, the grand story, we give to God.

In a sense, even reading this book is the product of a story that thrives in you because of your memories and experiences. You carry a story about reading, about how you learned and what you've experienced, as well as the value reading gives to your life and spirit.

Scripture is a story of people who have had experiences with God: memories of a bush that never burned up (Ex 3:3), walls that fell (Josh 6:20), and water transformed into a deep-red Cabernet with only a thought-whisper from Jesus (Jn 2:1-11). These memories are carried, conveyed around fires, valued, and taught from generation to generation. But even more than that, these stories become part of the human framework of each individual hearer.

Every person in Scripture lived out a personal story incarnated by an even greater story about God, life, and the world. That story came from the politics, theology, and culture ingrained in their memories through experiences. To be sure, our reading of Scripture is mining the memories of others.

To be an Israelite, for example, was to bear on your body—literally, in terms of circumcision for the men—the story of a God setting his people apart as unique and different. They lived differently because of that story.

To be a follower of Jesus was to engage the senses through tasting the wine and bread while smelling their richness and remembering the God who chose to serve his people rather than to first be served by them.

Each of these stories—which are corporate—was lived out, often without much thought to the origin of the actions. It is also true of our individual stories today. We are living in the way that our stories have formed us to live. As James Bryan Smith says, "Our stories are running our lives—in ways we may not even be aware of."[2]

These stories are all attached to a *cantus primus*—a specific theme or through line that traverses throughout the Bible and throughout all humanity.[3] This line of thinking asks, Who am I? Who is God? What happens when those two identities intersect? The Scriptures' answer is Jesus, who fulfills, fills, and envisions a world that we measure our stories and memories against.

Understanding how the biology of memory works helps us know that through the Spirit and presence of Jesus, we are formed as we write in the margins of this great *cantus primus* God has woven into the universe. The story of love, loss, redemption, and salvation begs us to write in the margins. Understanding our memories—and the stories they create—is a way God has given us to understand *how* we write in the margins every day.

WHOSE STORY IS THIS?

Some stories, however, have been handed down to us. For some, we were not yet cognizant, and for others, we weren't even born when experiences, memories, and stories affected our family and communities. We began to carry those stories in ourselves. In Deuteronomy the children of Israel carried a story of escape and liberation that they themselves never saw but was handed to them by parents and grandparents.

Today, the field of epigenetics is beginning to discover that emotional damage through experience—abuse or other trauma done to parents—can be passed on to their children genetically, creating a story they carry in their bodies as if they had experienced it themselves.[4]

Writer Elizabeth Rosner recounts a study by the epigeneticist Rachel Yehuda looking at the grandchildren and great-grandchildren of Holocaust survivors. Yehuda found post-traumatic stress disorder in Holocaust survivors' children and grandchildren that was "'inexplicable' by any other means than intergenerational transmission. Which is to say, my generation's DNA carries the *expression* of our parents' trauma, and the trauma of our grandparents too."[5]

Rosner summed up meeting adult children of Holocaust survivors (like herself) this way:

> Given the chance to listen, I found that although their stories sounded anything but identical to my own, the

tangled emotions they described suggested an unlikely yet compelling familiarity. Disproportionate burdens of grief, anxiety, rage, and so much more. Ghosts of experience that both did and did not seem to belong to us.[6]

Is it possible that our *memories* are also inherited? Part of our DNA? Is it possible that we carry a story within us that we "remember" only in the sense that those who raised us gave it to us as an inheritance? Imagine the generation of children whose parents died wandering in the wilderness after the miraculous exodus from Egypt. Memories were handed down—in their minds or their bodies—that they did not choose or seek out.

Yet the collected memories of their ancestors come to them and form them.

We all have these kinds of stories.

The situation grows complicated at this point. We're a mess of experiences, memories, and stories that come from assorted sources and make us a patchwork person. We are a bit of everything that has come before us, but within that patchwork is where God is active.

This is the main reason why our spiritual formation must include, for example, the way we deal with racism. Racism cannot be, as some would say, a "sin problem, not a skin problem," because the shells that we've inherited regarding race are built on *skin* and *sin*. Personal sin is certainly a factor in hatred, but the object of the hatred has more to do with cultural memory than with individual spiritual misdirection.

Anger and hate are within us. Our memories, stories, and scripts teach us to give anger and hate a "target."

The targets often come by the way we processed our experiences through the lenses of family and geography. They are informed by institutions, folk tales, films, and biases, which are handed down with little critical interpretation.

A joke or crude slur here or there? A shell goes into our hands. It came from a loving grandmother, grandfather, or institution we trust. The shell has value because of the value we give to the one presenting it to us, so it needs to be kept and treasured.

We will be forever hindered in our formation if we cannot begin to address our racial and gender stereotypes and biases from the perspective of, *Where did this shell come from, anyway?* God is present with us when we choose to join him in this critical work of radically and poetically reinterpreting our shells.

Jesus entered this kind of world—a world that was already brimming with experiences, memories, and the resulting stories. The memory of Roman cruelty and the story of the Roman occupation is a critical part of Jesus' world. He operated within that world for the sake of God's beautiful redemption and formation of his people.

It must be this way.

All memories, and all remembering for that matter, are a form of storytelling.

We form the stories about ourselves, the world, and others out of the things we have stored in the deep recesses of our brains. Then, because the stories are alive in us, we begin to *script* our lives within them. That shaping is where we find the intersection of our own lives and the "spirit of Christ being formed" in us (Gal 4:19, my paraphrase).

WE ARE PEOPLE WITH A SCRIPT

Author Barbara Brown Taylor recounts her first experience with caving, the exploration of caves that are not prepared or made easily accessible for inexperienced explorers.

All memories, and all remembering for that matter, are a form of storytelling.

Her guides gave her a bit of helpful advice. As you move forward, continue to look back so that you can memorize not only the front of the rocks you pass but also the back sides. To leave the cave, you need to know what it looks like where you came from.[7]

To know where we are, we have to know the script of how we got there in the first place.

The question from our earlier discussion still remains: Why do we do what we do? You woke this morning and immediately began to do something—perhaps it was a *little* something, done slowly, measuring each step because before coffee you are a danger to yourself and others. Your memories—whether implicit or nondeclarative—began to act without your permission but for your wellness and functionality.

Maybe you didn't wake up looking for your clothes, as I did, but you had operating instructions that intuitively kicked in.

Perhaps you gave thought to your actions—turning the faucet handle or the side-to-side motion of buttering toast—as you put on the soft mantle of your responsibilities for the day.

We wake to operate out of a *script* already written in our memories. It has been formed in us, and we are in turn formed by it as we move through each day.

In terms of spiritual formation, we wake up and ask, *How am I going to change today?* or *How might I experience God today?* We rarely ask, *How did I come to the habits and actions I'm taking today?* To ask the latter question is the gift of memories in our formation; it allows us to see the landmarks we passed on the way to the present moment.

We are people who gather experiences that become memories, and those memories create stories we integrate into our mind, body, and soul. Then we begin to live in the flow of their presence.

Since our time of gathering shells in the Caribbean, my family and I act and think by a different script. We tell stories that begin with "Remember Bob the lizard?" or "How can we get back there?" We've even gone so far as to think about church planting—which I am not gifted for or called to do—in the Caribbean just so we could go back and stay in that near-Eden land.

People on beaches need churches too, right? Or at least a spiritual director?

FLIPPING SCRIPTS

Our script originates from the stories we've gathered regarding where we belong in the world, who we are, and also who we are *not*. Our memories and stories have given us source material for shaping our identity. As Mike Yaconelli says, "A sad reality of modern life is the increasing number of people whose past abuse has convinced them of their unworthiness."[8]

Success without correction or challenge suggests that we're impenetrable. An experience with a graceless follower of Jesus has confirmed our suspicion that God has put us on the "naughty list," never to be removed. Then we live out our lives accordingly.

When it comes to our formation into Christlikeness, the script conversation crackles with life. Paul writes, "Once you were darkness, but now in the Lord you are light" (Eph 5:8). This isn't merely stating some observable fact, this is telling a far different tale of our lives.

In other words, remember who you are, and since that's true— *here are your stage directions*. Here is your *script*. Our identity comes from the stories told by our memories, and those stories— that identity—will shape who we are and how we act. And we often need to be reminded of this.

God's poetic activity in our lives is incredibly rich when it comes to the scripts we follow. How we walk creates either ripples of hope or tidal waves of ache and disappointment, and scripts are where our formation work often focuses. The spiritual practice of remembering is the way we make sense of this very human experience of gathering shells in the presence of God.

In fact, most of our teaching in the Christian tradition revolves around *editing the script*. Changing our behavior, in this view, is the finishing move of our transformation. The experience of reading Scripture even presents us with the challenge to choke off the dark and destructive behaviors (see Col 3:5) we carry due to experiences and memories that form life-hindering stories and scripts.

While I don't disagree with that idea, my experience is that the process is not that simple. Editing the script is only effective if we take time to understand, with the guidance of God's Spirit, what this life of collecting shells has built into us.

If in our script we abuse our bodies, we may take steps to stem the tide. We decide to eat better, quit anything that we do to excess, or think about our sexual habits and behaviors in a different light. None of this is wrong, however it simply doesn't go far enough.

When Paul says the opposite of conformity is not being radical but being "transformed by the renewing of your minds" (Rom 12:2), I believe he is pulling at the hidden thread of it all.

Renewing our minds means understanding the hidden structure of the way we think, feel, and operate. Naturally, our memories are part of that process. Then we work backward: The script is only present because of the *story*. The story grows from our *memories*, which, as we know, begin as *experiences*.

We will live with Jesus—whether we desire it this way or not—only as deeply and pervasively as the stories we've gathered will allow us to go. Our scripts are born from our stories. Even our shifts in behavior will only take full flight if we begin to grasp the "therefore" of a passage like Colossians 3:5.

> *We will live with Jesus—whether we desire it this way or not—only as deeply and pervasively as the stories we've gathered will allow us to go.*

Transformation truly begins only when we read Colossians 3:5 while remembering a *new* story, namely, "If you have been raised with Christ, seek the things that are above, where Christ is, seated at the right hand of God. Set your minds on things that are above, not on things that are on earth, for you have died, and your life is hidden with Christ in God" (Col 3:1-3).

GOD IS PRESENT THROUGH THE PROCESS

Gathering experiences, solidifying memories, crafting stories, and moving with the script are all places where God is present and active. He sees them as they are, and the promised Spirit of Jesus moves gently and wisely toward both the strong points and the weak spaces in our collection of shells. He sees the rough-edged, shattered, coarse fragments and the fully formed, color-blessed shells that we choose to present to anyone who would look.

God is always present in our memories, but we are often absent.

What if the next and most critical step on our road of formation is to actively encounter the living and vibrant God in and among our memories? The God who is present to our pain, who cheers the moments of perseverance and patience—what if he is inviting us to a moment of reflection, engagement, and even reenvisioning of the shells we've gathered thus far?

It may seem daunting to engage with God regarding our memories because so much of our lives is on a forward trajectory. But if we see the process of gathering shells clearly, we'll notice that we show up to our memories every day in the form of stories and scripts that shape how we live.

The spiritual practice of remembering—the practice of engaging with God in our memories—is refusing to passively receive our story and script up to this point, and instead actively embracing God's presence and our humanity in the midst of it.

As adults we return to our childhood memories and engage with God there. We see the way our stories and scripts were shaped and humbly say, "God, help me rewrite what is broken and shortsighted."

As a spouse, we return to memories of our parents' marriage or our own sexual and relational struggles and say, "God redeem these things that now cling to me like chains."

The journey forward in our formation, our living deeply in the kingdom as apprentices of Jesus, is also a journey backward to find those shells that have shaped and seasoned our lives to become what they are today.

What shells have you gathered?

What stories and scripts emerge as you run your fingers over the edges?

Where is God present among those shells—and where is he inviting you to be present as well?

PRACTICE

Every great stage play, drama, comedy series, or movie has an over-arching story and a script that leads the performers and crew toward bringing a narrative to life. In this chapter, we see memories turn into stories and scripts that become the overarching narratives in our lives.

This practice asks that we take a memory—either one we've already identified or another memory that comes to mind—and imagine it as a production with a story and a script. In this practice the hope is to be able to reimagine our memories by looking at the factors that created those memories in the first place.

- Begin by bringing a memory to mind and think about the *who*, *what*, *when*, and *where* of the memory. These are parts of the setting, and they all contribute to the story and script of your memory. As they come to you, you may want to write all the details in a journal so you can refer to them later. Make sure to include God or the Spirit of Jesus (whichever feels the most comfortable to you) in the *who* of your memory.

- The story of your memory is the main theme—it can typically be stated in one sentence such as "The time I _____" or "When my _____" or "When I experienced _____." State the main theme of your memory in one sentence.

- While there is a big-picture theme, each element of your memory (specifically each individual) includes multiple stories, including the "shells" of the people involved in your life up to this point. Looking at the people in your memory, including yourself and God, state in one sentence each person's individual story at the time of the memory. For example, you may say, "Dad: Struggled with alcoholism and came from an abusive family" or "Mom: Caring and compassionate but feared confrontation." Create a story line for each individual.

- In good productions, the story then shapes the script. Characters speak, act, or relate in certain ways because of their stories. Now that you have thought about the stories of the people in your memory, look at the script of your memory (what everyone did or said) and meditate on how their stories affected their scripts.

- Take a moment in prayer to remember God is present in the story of your memory. Ask him to help you as you reflect on the story, stories, and scripts of your memory. Listen for any steps you may need to take toward those in your memory, such as forgiving, confronting, or even creating space between you for the sake of spiritual and emotional health.

- If you are keeping a journal, write a reflection on this practice, noting things you heard and questions that came up that you'll need to pursue.

4

THE WEIGHT OF SHELLS

The mind is its own place, and in itself, can make a heaven of hell, a hell of heaven.

JOHN MILTON

We once lived in a house that was the patchwork of a structure from the 1950s with an addition from the 1990s. The house had strange idiosyncrasies like light switches that did nothing and others that turned on appliances in rooms in totally different parts of the house. Occasionally when running the vacuum and the microwave at the same time, every light in the house would dim to a mood-setting glow.

When repair people came—plumbers, electricians, and carpenters—we'd often hear them utter the same refrain, "Well, huh." We also heard, "Wow, that's interesting." We'd even hear, "Why would they do it that way?" It was a unique house, and we were often suspicious when new creaks or clicks made their presence known.

We dreaded service calls. We knew that once the repair person took down the drywall or uncovered the electrical wiring, we would find more than a simple problem waiting to be solved.

Spiritual formation, as I defined it earlier, is becoming like Jesus within our skin. Of course, it is skin with history. To live in this skin—or in the drywall in the case of a house—we have to explore what makes it, what makes us, who we are. We need to see underneath the weathered layers to the generative life underneath, not only the life God created and sustained but also the life we have stewarded and fumbled along the way.

I believe there are bold and brilliant possibilities for redemption while we're in this skin, driving toward what Frank Laubach calls "undiscovered continents of spiritual living compared with which we are infants in arms."[1]

The obstacle to living in our own skin is, of course, accurately seeing what's underneath. To explore our memories is to be able to use our gift of hindsight to see what's behind the drywall, so to speak.

BOLDLY GOING BACKWARD

Redemption always requires the faithful courage to face things that are brittle and dysfunctional.

When we pull out the jar of shells, we sort through them and see the realities of moments long gone by. We pause to pray, perhaps asking God to flush our minds and shatter the shells that scratched us and continue to do so. Perhaps we pray that we might capture that time with a spouse or family member, that lightning-in-a-bottle moment, when everything conformed to a sitcom-styled perfection. We long for those moments when conversations were natural and tinged with grace instead of pregnant with suspicion and contempt.

We see the shells and notice that some are small and delicate and have an oil-slicked surface where we see our own reflection. We then notice that some are large and imposing, and their weight threatens to crush those small and beautiful moments we hold so dearly. They may be visually beautiful, but their presence is intimidating.

We pray for grace from God, for wisdom and insight, and then sometimes we pray to forget. We ask for these shells to disappear. We want to leave them behind the drywall.

We need to explore some broader realities about the spiritual practice of remembering before we can fully grasp the challenges ahead of us as we engage with God to revise our scripts.

Or sometimes we simply lose track of events and experiences. Sometimes we banish them into the darkness because we believe they are best left where they can rot and die. The unkind word, the passing comment, the deed left undone—we are convinced that they are no longer valuable and must be left behind for us to move on.

Yet they stay. Do you have a shell that fits here? One that you would rather toss into the retreating tide, never to be seen again? Bring it to mind now—hold it—look at it despite all the resistance you feel. Despite our best efforts, it remains. Most interesting, though, someone else is abiding alongside that moment as well. We with him, and he with us (see Jn 15). Of course, that doesn't make the confrontation of those shells any easier for us.

If we are going to see our memories as part of our formation, it requires that we understand the obstacles that arise when we begin to think about our memories. The obstacles of distaste, neglect, or simply confusion remove us from what could be a life-giving and strengthening practice.

This is only one perspective on why we look away from the past (and our memories) in every area of life, including spiritual formation. We need to explore some broader realities about the spiritual practice of remembering before we can fully grasp the challenges ahead of us as we engage with God to revise our scripts.

MEMORIES ARE COMPLICATED

We have a tense relationship with the past, and many times it feels easier to simply let it slip into the fog of irrelevance. Writer Margaret Bendroth goes further, saying there are three predominant cultural assumptions about time gone by:

1. The past is "behind" us.

2. The past is inferior to the present.

3. The past is not really *real*.[2]

To be sure, many of us may agree with at least the first two assumptions, and for a very good reason. If we have lived through a difficult season that we wish not to reflect on, if we have experienced a life change via the transformation of Christian faith, or if we simply are healthier and wiser with age than with youth, we might affirm that the past is best left behind. The third is a bit harder to agree to.

As we are finding, however, nothing collected through experience escapes value in our life with God. Jean-Pierre de Caussade says, "The will of God is the presence, the reality, and the virtue in all things, adjusting them to souls. Without God's direction, all is void, emptiness, vanity, words, superficiality, death."[3]

To make the past irrelevant is actually dangerous because to eliminate the past is to eliminate the stories and scripts that shape us into the moment when we engage with God. All memories are flush with the presence of God; we must choose to meet him there. Of course, we always meet him there. We can't do anything other than meet God where he is *as we are*.

In his transparent and moving journal *The Inner Voice of Love*, Henri Nouwen talks about growth (or healing) and says, "Your healing is not a straight line. You must expect setbacks and regressions."[4] So the crooked line behind us will give us wisdom for the weaving way ahead.

To remember anything well is to reengage the moment in its fullness. It is to press through the fog, whether through talking with others or through revisiting journals and places of significance, to the heart of what has gone by.

To remember well is also to see that our healing could be a lifelong process, not a weekend retreat. Jesus is a companion for journeys and will be present with us throughout our encounter with our complicated past. It is not easy work to remember well; it's so difficult that Jesus promises the divine Spirit to go with us—the *paraklete* or "one who comes alongside" (Jn 14:16-17, 26) to not only be with us but to teach and *remind* us.

Remember who you are.

Remember you are not alone.

You are, as James Bryan Smith says, "one in whom Christ dwells and delights."[5]

Often it is the fear of going into our memories alone that petrifies us. It keeps us standing with eyes facing forward, hoping that what has gone before never makes a reappearance even though we feel the cold breath of the past on our shoulder.

Or perhaps we have banished memories of past successes for the sake of avoiding complacency or achieving some sort of false humility where we testify to God, "I haven't done much for you lately." We want to avoid what Jim Collins calls "the hubris born of success," which breeds dishonesty and overconfidence, but at the same time we also want to avoid seeing the successes of the past that appear like strangers to us in the present.[6]

In both cases we must learn how, in the sweet Spirit and presence of God, to engage the complicated nature of our memories. It often begins with stripping wallpaper and pulling nails.

JOSEPH'S BROTHERS COME CLEAN

The process of remembering is painful because it requires a courageous interaction with a past reality. Often our most painful memories are of *passive* events—ones where we were the victim, where we bore the weight of consequences. Of course, there is also a category of painful memories containing *active* events, ones in which we set the events in motion and now walk with the scent of regret in our nostrils.

Sometimes our shells are broken.

Sometimes we broke them.

And sometimes it is a convergence of both, of active and passive pain.

Memories are complicated because as we look at them we see our own viewpoint, and with the complement of time we see the point of view of others. Imagine Joseph, the young son of Isaac in the Genesis story, sitting down with his brothers long after settling their affairs and bringing the family to live in Egypt (Gen 42–45). Did they ever have a conversation that went like this? "Joseph, we're really sorry for beating you up and throwing you in the well. And, yes, we're sorry for selling you into slavery."

Joseph tilts his head and says, "Even though you *intended* to do harm to me, God *intended* it for good, in order to preserve a numerous people, as he is doing today" (Gen 50:20, emphasis added).

Joseph, the wonderer and dreamer who should have understood the jealousy of siblings, meets his brothers who beat him and sold him into slavery, and engages that memory with redemption.

The Hebrew word translated "intended" at the root means "to weave"—it is the process of taking what *is* and making it into beautiful.[7]

Joseph pauses to scratch his head. Then he says, "So why did you do that to me, anyway?"

With the benefit of age and time, Joseph starts to see the situation differently, and the brothers begin to talk about Joseph's boasting and claiming that they were going to bow at his feet.

"It got annoying, honestly," they say.

Joseph suddenly has a picture of the situation that he didn't have before, "Wait, so I put some of this stuff in motion?"

This is a completely fictional conversation, but it is the kind of formation conversation that we—and the biblical figures we know and love—have access to if we are willing to *remember*. If we are willing to reenter moments long past and begin to peel back the layers of details to reveal the structure underneath, Joseph points out a way of engagement.

When we remember as a part of our formation journey we see patterns, hang-ups, responses, and sins that alienate us from the person we were created to be. David extends an invitation to God to "Search me, O God, and know my heart" (Psalm 139:23), which is, in fact, an invitation to explore motivations both past and present to get at the wealth of wisdom that lies underneath.

Like any renovation or repair, we begin with the dust and the demolition, but we end with something fresh and clean. Paint. Light fixtures. Carpet. But for many of us, the demolition seems far too painful to even start the renovation.

It brings us to a place of confession, both to God and others, and while confession is the alcohol swab that cleanses the skin for vaccination, we still hesitate to present ourselves to that moment. Confession is the critical move we make on our memories because it is an engagement with God *as well as* our own selves. As David Seamands remarks, "We cannot confess to God what we do not acknowledge to ourselves."[8]

There are several memories that I return to on a regular basis. There are failures, missteps, and outright selfishness that color the canvas of my evolving forty years on this planet. I may be driving, waiting in a doctor's office, or in a meeting when I find myself transported backward to that moment in time.

I watch as the scene or scenes unfold—they show completed events, so I am a spectator to my own actions. I feel I can do nothing. I can only see myself and my motives, watching words flow and wanting desperately to capture them in a glass jar and bury them deep in the ground never to be seen again.

Yet it happened as it happened.

When I suggest that one of the obstacles to remembering is that we do not want to see what lies behind the drywall, I am setting up a nonexistent situation. The reality is that for the most critical memories—the ones that really sting us or fill us with regret—we can do nothing *but* remember.

There is a way of forgetting that affirms Elizabeth Rosner's definition of forgetting: "Forgetting . . . which both is and is not the opposite of Remembering."[9] We want to simply nail the drywall back up, toss the shells in the garbage, and enter into a mythical place that many call moving on. More than that, we believe God desires this from us also. Forgive and forget or, in the language of memory, forgetting ourselves and our stories.

FORGIVE BUT DON'T FORGET

We cannot begin the journey of spiritual formation pretending that what is behind our drywall really isn't there. We do not start with a blank slate; we are never formed outside the script we currently live by.

That problematic phrase lives here: *forgive and forget.* While there is destructive power in letting a past failure or experience of hurt govern our lives, there is also great poverty in believing we can completely erase this experience, and therefore our stories and scripts, from our memories.

We read and salivate over texts like this one in Isaiah:

Do not remember the former things,
    or consider the things of old.
I am about to do a new thing;
    now it springs forth, do you not perceive it? (Is 43:18-19)

We see the failure behind the drywall, and we long to forget the former things. New things, *yes,* bring on the new things. The past is a wearying prospect.

Someone then says, "Yes, your past does not define you." Yet as we have seen, the past most definitely defines us because it creates the context—the memories, stories, and scripts—that makes us who we are. God is doing a new thing, certainly, but he is doing it in an old us.

In terms of our formation in Christ, it seems better to say, "Your past does not *determine* you." It does not set the finality, the terminus, of our life and formation. It does not end our journey of becoming.

It isn't "forgive and forget," but instead, "Forgive and learn to remember differently."

A man named Paul comes to mind. Trained by the brightest of Jewish teachers, zealous beyond zeal, the former Saul created a train of shells that included persecution, arrest, and approval of the execution of followers of Jesus, the people of the Way.

Then Paul is—as many of us are—blindsided with his own reality and shown his shells by Jesus. He is invited to stop his crusade, blinded, and humbled to a place of dependency on others (Acts 9:1-9). How accurately this describes the scenes that dot many of our memories and stories!

He turns his zeal, then, toward this blinding vision of Jesus. He is baptized and receives his sight, goes into the wilderness for an extended period of solitude, and then returns to meet with the leaders of this community of Jesus followers. He was walking toward those who at one point felt the heat of his "breathing threats and murder" (Acts 9:1) from across the Sea of Galilee.

They do not forget his past.

However, someone vouches for Saul-now-Paul and a new journey begins.

Yet, as we read the story of Paul, we recognize one salient thing: *no one ever forgot about Saul.* Was there forgiveness? Certainly. Did anyone forget what happened prior to Damascus or during the stoning of Stephen? No. Mainly because *Paul never forgot those moments and talked about them frequently.* For example, "If anyone else has reason to be confident in the flesh, I have more: circumcised on the eighth day, a member of the people of Israel, of the tribe of Benjamin, a Hebrew born of Hebrews; as to the law, a Pharisee; as to zeal, a persecutor of the church; as to righteousness under the law, blameless" (Phil 3:4-6).

Reading his laundry list of "accomplishments"—including persecuting the followers of the Way—you get the sense that they are in no way *forgotten.* They simply are no longer *actionable.* Paul has left behind his former ideals and sees those moments in a different light. They are remembered but are redeemed by being put in their proper place: "Yet whatever gains I had, these I have come to regard as loss because of Christ" (Phil 3:7).

Paul's "regard" could also be translated "consider." Both require bringing forward an idea or event, placing it on the laboratory table, and pulling it apart to see the intricate weavings within.

To consider our memories is to examine them, to see them as they are, to remember them as they are, and then to consider them differently in the light of the formation journey we are invited to in Christ.

To peer behind the drywall of our lives and see the memories, stories, and scripts that form the context of who we are means we will need to discover with Jesus the formation path that allows us to both remember and redeem the context of our stories. We consider them from a new perspective.

THE JOURNEY OF REDEMPTION

What we need most in the moments when we enter our complicated memories and pull back the drywall to discover what is underneath is the *redemption* of our memories. Moments we have considered worthless or even harmful are suddenly given value by the God who heals—the God who lives not in calendar time with its various demands but in *kairos* time, which is best described as nonchronological sacredness.

This is where the idea of leaving the past behind or not letting it define us fails to give us the relief and restoration we so desperately need.

My daughter, now well past the kid-snickering phase, will still chuckle quietly when *The Lion King*'s Pumbaa the warthog opines, "You gotta put your *behind* in your past."

It is difficult to find those who would disagree with Pumbaa's direction here. As present- and future-focused people, the role relegated to the past is typically sentimental and nostalgic. We keep the high school picture or letter jacket, but we leave behind much of everything else. We do it out of contempt. We also do it for the sake of survival.

When we survey our story, we will notice a moment when we were wounded deeply. People we trusted abused or abandoned us at the time when we needed them the most, and what they left was a deep chasm in our story. It has made us who we are today.

We decide who to allow into our lives based on this event.

We decide which relationships we will pursue in the present because of this painful moment in the past.

We have an implicit story about our value and worth to the world based on the emotional impact of this past event. It has reshaped us at the most fundamental levels.

We have Pavlovian memories: earthy, visceral, and primitive, strikingly different from more factual, intellectual recollections.

Persons who have been in a serious automobile accident "may later react to screeching brakes with a racing heart, sweaty palms, and a surge of adrenaline."[10]

Unchecked, these shells become memories that dominate us, and our story gnarls like a Zinfandel vine. But instead of giving us beautiful hardiness to withstand the elements, it creates a fragile script of bitterness, ache, and disappointment. This is neither the life that Jesus calls "abundant" (Jn 10:10) nor is it equal to that station we were created for.

REDEEMING AND ASSOCIATING

The robbing of our lives occurs when the core story of who we are—created as "very good" (Gen 1:31) and never downgraded, and "beloved" of God (1 Jn 3:2)—is taken through specific memories and twisted into something far more sinister than any demon possession.

Bessel van der Kolk, known for his legendary work on trauma and the body, notes our minds disassociate with traumatic events by putting them in "frozen, barely comprehensible fragments."[11]

We may have memories attached to a certain place, smell, or song. They seem far away or absent at times but are still beneath the surface pushing our stories and scripts into the present and future. We choose what to do with the drywall.

Dr. van der Kolk continues, "If the problem with PTSD is *dissociation*, the goal of treatment would be *association*: integrating the cut-off elements into the ongoing narrative of life."[12]

While we may not suffer clinical levels of trauma, we all find ways to distance ourselves from memories that cause us pain. In turn, we are also invited by Jesus to carry our belovedness into our memories and allow him to heal and reintegrate those elements we'd rather leave behind into a life of graceful formation. Our identity becomes the partnership with God that we take into our exploration of pain, passion, perseverance, and pensive moments. This is the ground of redemption for our memories.

When it comes to our painful memories, we long for amnesia, but we need redemption and reintegration.

Healing our memories and redeeming past events for the sake of future formation is not about reaching a point of worthiness but beginning from a status of belovedness and hiddenness (Col 3:3) that only Jesus can provide. Robert Mulholland says, "It is clear that the only valid context for our inner reorientation and striving is the fact that 'you have died, and your life is hidden with Christ in God.'"[13]

> *When it comes to our painful memories, we long for amnesia, but what we need is redemption and reintegration.*

Jesus centers us not only within the present but within the past. He orients us toward things that we cannot change in order to be present with us in them, redeeming them as we hold them out to him. Remembering is the practice of bringing our memories forward and engaging them in the presence of God.

Memories must be redeemed—and to be redeemed they have to be embraced just as they are, just where they are without gloss or ceremony, or else they become demons emboldened to pull back on the reins of our lives at will.

Of course, past pain has a spiritual impact. If we look at the spiritual life as the work of the mind (the way we process the world), the heart (the will and energy for us to do what we do), and the hands (our active movements in everyday life), it isn't difficult to see how a past pain significantly shapes our spiritual lives.

To redeem our memories, we must begin where we are least likely to go, the place that we feel is least relevant in the here and now. Yet we can never truly leave our "behind" in our past. Our formation in the future is waiting for the redemption of the memories, stories, and scripts that trail behind.

PAUSE

Take a moment and let the quiet of your surroundings overcome you. If you aren't in a quiet place, come back to this practice later when you have some control over the noise level of your environment.

Remember, God is with you. He has promised to never leave you or forsake you, so he is immediately and intimately present in this moment.

Settle into this moment and ask this question: *Is there a memory I am avoiding today—something behind the drywall that I don't want to acknowledge?*

Sit in the silence and let this memory come forward. Respond to it by letting it be, knowing that God will care for you in its presence.

Listen for anything God may have to say to you as you look at this memory.

5

EVERY MEMORY BELONGS

God is waiting for us. He is accepting the gift we make.
He has entered into time for us, to show us what time is.

EMILIE GRIFFIN

I once returned to my hometown to visit my grandparents, aunts, and numerous cousins. I drove the route by myself for the first time and found it odd that after being a passenger for so many years, I still didn't have a clear understanding of how to get there.

The route came to me, however. I passed the jail, then the board of education. I headed up the hill and eventually made a left. The streets grew more and more narrow, which I knew from navigating them on a bike, but not in a car. How strange to realize that though I knew the way, when it came time to take it, I grew nervous and insecure. The alley that ran behind my grandparents' house felt like a narrow slit, and I wondered if my car could actually keep four wheels on pavement.

Surviving the tightening gauntlet of homes and ditches, I pulled into the gravel parking spot and made my way down the hill.

I found my grandparents' house with the same black metal awning, the same stone path through the backyard, and in many ways it was the same house on Thomas Street where I spent Sunday after Sunday of my childhood. Despite a decade or so having passed, a plastic bat and ball were still tucked neatly under the awning's falling edge.

I pressed the latch.

I opened the door.

Everything was different. My four cousins had all brought children of their own into the story, making the house feel smaller than I remembered. I was now an adult, but it still felt as if time had slowly compressed the walls. The smells were the same. The toys strewn about were different, and I sat in an adult chair and had adult conversations rather than scampering back out to head up the alley and through the yards. I drank coffee instead of lemonade. I talked about legislation rather than Little League.

It was the same.

It was not the same.

I felt a small pang of grief as I mixed my memories of growing up with my new experience of sitting in that living room. *I'd rather go back*, I thought. Back to the childhood moments when my parents were only troubled, not divorced. Back before I had made relational mistakes and wounded the hearts of many I cared about. I also felt a warm and welcome invitation to go back to the days before I kept my distance from that hometown and busied myself with the work of moving on. It was, however, impossible.

"You can never go home again," according to an old adage.

I disagree. You can go home again, but it would be best if you moderated your expectations.

Our memories and the scripts they create fill our souls with moments like these. Sometimes they happen in a funeral home, sometimes they come as we look at a photo album, and sometimes they come when we are sitting in a chair, winding our words around a prayerful conversation with God.

Or they come when you see the temple again for the first time.

A STRANGE THING HAPPENED IN EZRA

There is a story in the book of Ezra, perhaps one of the most interesting memories in the history of Israel. I call this story, "When Things Went Back to Normal . . . Kinda." The story of Israel began with a promise, one of hope, of a land where they would dwell in safety with God and engage a law that brought order and life to their world (Gen 17:1-8; Ex 19:5 for example).

The story was bumpy from that point on. Halfhearted attempts to live with God and others, moments of sublime faith and stupendous failure, and ultimately a season of exile dotted the memories of the people. The script was one of struggle.

I can relate to that story. I believe we all can.

In Ezra and Nehemiah, two companion books of the Old Testament, the story of homecoming begins. The people are restored to the great city Jerusalem, filled with history and memories of its own. There is a rebuilding process—almost as if a resurrection takes place.

We should step back and place ourselves in this story.

The scene in Ezra that has always captured my attention is one where the temple is rebuilt. The temple forms the center of their script, drawing both from the memories of their great-great-great-grandparents, who wandered out of Egypt and met God in a tent, and those of the wise king Solomon, who built a mar-velous temple in which God's presence could dwell. (This was right before Solomon's modern-day celebrity flameout with wives who worshiped devious gods, of course.)

In the exile prior to Ezra and Nehemiah, the temple was deci-mated, and with it went a major part of Israel's script. *If God is not in the neighborhood, then our roots have been removed.*

The comfort of presence is replaced with the pain of longing that would not—at least while they were walking in Babylon—be satisfied.

It is the same pain we experience when a friend, spouse, or parent has died.

It is the sharp sting of a relationship that, though the person still lives and breathes and frequents the same grocery store, will never be repaired because of a word or action. It is the waking of a demon in our spirit and indulging that incorrigible addiction that separates us from family and friends. It is a memory alive with ache, often waking us from a dead sleep.

The return came for Israel, and there was great joy. They came back to the city and rebuilt it, and in the process they laid the foundation for a new temple. There was something else in the air however, like a minor chord that created dissonance in the major key. I imagine Israelite wives scrambling to put together their finest clothes and foods to celebrate the day they returned to the temple, the day God returned to the temple.

Imagine that your relational wounds were suddenly re-versed, healed, and repaired. Imagine that grace and for-giveness overcame the wounding that your addiction created. Imagine a great button was pressed that deleted your words of selfishness and harm, and things moved back toward the way they used to be.

Wouldn't there still be something hanging in the air? Something haunting that moment?

The day comes for Israel when they unveil the temple's foundation, and something strange happens.

> All the people responded with a great shout when they praised the LORD, because the foundation of the house of the LORD was laid. But many of the priests and Levites and heads of families, old people who had seen the first house on its foundations, *wept* with a loud voice when they saw this house, though *many shouted aloud for joy,* so that the people *could not distinguish* the sound of the joyful shout from the sound of the people's weeping, for the people shouted so loudly that the sound was heard far away. (Ezra 3:11-13, emphasis added)

Their memories collided with present-day reality. Homecoming and remembrances of the first temple grappled with each other. Joy at the present and future danced with the grief of the past. Memories of my grandparents' house whispered in my ear as I looked around with adult eyes. When we engage our memories with God, it is often difficult to distinguish weeping from cheering; in fact, they may be taking place simultaneously.

When we step into the journey of following Jesus through the script our memories have made, we must realize that every memory belongs.

When we step into the journey of following Jesus through the script our memories have made, we must realize that *every memory belongs.*

MEMORIES UNSEEN

Sitting across the table from Jeff, we talked about life. He was the executive director of a local nonprofit, and he had reached out to get to know me.

As we talked, he shared his family's journey of the last few years. A difficult church situation, a miscarriage, and the discovery of a niche where he and his family could live and serve were all part of the narrative.

As he shared this story, I thought about the reality of pain. Throughout my life, I've been challenged by the notion that God allows pain. When sitting with parents who have just lost a child, stillborn or even later, we see the face of pain. The reality of a newly married woman who faithfully served her community and built beautiful relationships with every person she met only to be struck with an aneurysm and die shortly after her wedding forces us to see the pale and barren ground of pain.

Yet pain is *part* of the story. Memories of pain shape us most directly and incisively. If I were to ask ten people to recount their most vivid memory, the one that has the greatest impact on them still today, I would wager the majority would recount a painful memory. Whether we can reconcile the theology of pain or not, the impact of pain is significant to the formation of the spirit and soul.

So as Jeff and I listened to coffee beans grinding and felt the waves and punctuations of other conversations around us, I tried to paint a picture about pain for my friend. I don't believe God causes pain, and to say God allows it is only a way of speaking about a reality that we can't grasp completely.

God is over all creation (Ps 8:1), but that is also a cloudy understanding—an incomplete picture. We process the idea of being "over" something through our corporate or military lens. To us it means that God is in control of it all, calling every shot and moving every chess piece into play.

The Scriptures paint a different picture, however. God is seen as one, but we also see the developing story of Trinity, diversity in oneness. God is not one who "change[s] like shifting shadows" (Jas 1:17 NIV), but he also listens to Moses and relents from destroying the Hebrews in the desert. God is *over* pain by being *present* within it.

God, who is incarnate, who is with us in Jesus, dwells in the complications of our memories as well.

The thought or picture of a needlepoint hoop came to me in that coffee shop. I had watched my mom craft needlepoint designs in the past, holding the wooden circle with the material stretched and tight in the center. The front, or the top, was a colorful image or script. Laid out well, it would line up and be able to be used as the cover for a pillow or something similar.

However, when we turn the hoop over, we see a garbled mess of knots and loops and colors. We also see that there are dark, muted colors mixed in with fresh and light colors.

The way we see our memories is the same. A present moment is vibrant and colorful, but if we look carefully and turn the hoop over, we'll also see a mess. We'll see the darker shades of pain, failure, and trauma woven into the bright colors of hope, forgiveness, and redemption.

Richard Rohr says, "Because the rational mind cannot process love or suffering, for example, it tends to either avoid them, deny them, or blame somebody for them, when in fact they are the greatest spiritual teachers of all, if we but allow them."[1]

The deepest work of our spiritual lives is this: reconciling the reality and goodness that have come through the interplay of the beautiful, the painful, and the mundane memories of our lives. It is to pray that every memory belongs.

WHERE WE'RE HEADED

That we can reach into our past and find things that *were* there or *already* happened means that we've moved forward. We may have done so with a bit of a limp, and we may have done so in spite of some very difficult circumstances, but we have moved forward nonetheless. Richard Rohr again is helpful here, "Unless you can chart and encourage both movement and direction, you have no way to name maturity or immaturity."[2] To chart is to intentionally remember, to return with anxiety and grace and find the movement hidden in the muddle.

> *The deepest work of our spiritual lives is this: reconciling the reality and goodness that have come through the interplay of the beautiful, the painful, and the mundane memories of our lives.*

We have come through physical abuse, carrying scars and fears and anxieties, but we are here. We stand alive.

We have come through the disappointment of not reaching our dreams and visions for what the good life might be, but we have some food and a place to live now. We stand alive and present.

We fought disease, and though we feel the effects of a sapped immune system and the lost time when we were incapacitated, we now have stories to tell and hope to give.

Movement is what transformation is made of—moving from one place to another, from one form to another, from one way of walking in the world to another. Yet there are some, and I find myself in this category from time to time, who wonder if the transformation of pain is even possible.

Henri Nouwen's great work *The Wounded Healer* is an exercise in memory, in knowing our frailties and limitations and allowing those to become healing agents in the world.[3] The Lord explains to the apostle Paul, "Power is made perfect in weakness" (2 Cor 12:9), and that resonates with us today as we think through our own memories.

When we embrace that every memory belongs and everything can be woven into something beautiful, we end up moving toward others who are in the midst of stifling scripts and immovable memories. We can help them see that every memory belongs. Like midwives, we can be present for the birth of something beautiful.

In a sense, our reckoning with everything in our memories allows us to flesh out "Love your neighbor as yourself" (Mt 22:39). For example, having lived through the divorce of my parents, I take that memory into every marriage-counseling session I engage in as a pastor. This is helpful in that I can speak to the experience of children and somewhat to the experience of couples going through that season. It is also challenging because not every marriage I encounter is the same as my parents'. The couple in front of me has their own script, their own stories, both separately and now together, that they need to engage and embrace.

Yet at the bottom, marriage entails engaging the story of where one has come from and allowing that story to merge with another's. In the process we assess what each person puts in the place of ultimate value. In other words, it doesn't take long after the ceremony to figure out what matters most to our spouse. We see it in how we fight, spend money, and value the opinion of our partner.

Where have we found places of weakness—places where our strength and resolve are sagging—and how have we responded? In this inquiry we find out what matters most to us, what belongs and what doesn't.

What has strength looked like? Have we found it in late nights sitting by a hospital bed, crying and praying in one fast-moving stream? Like the question about weakness, in our strength we find what matters most to us as well.

Questions of both weakness and strength *belong* because, in our formation journey with Jesus, every memory belongs.

THIS IS FOR YOU

Years ago I was teaching my daughter to ride her bike—a pink princess bike, I might add. With the training wheels long gone, she fought with balance and turns. I knew that with enough repetitions, with enough driveway time, she would master the art.

But, as with me, difficult things become frustrating.

She didn't want to keep riding. She wanted to get off and go do something else. She was tired of wobbling but not of falling off. She wanted to ride, but not today. I wanted her to stop resisting and keep trying until the muscle memory fastened itself deep within her. She laid the bike down, refusing to pedal, and I let the following escape my mental filter: "I do not have time to teach little babies how to ride bikes!"

She winced. I winced. Time was of the essence because I often worked six days a week. Her lips curled together and the tears were visible from a distance. "I am not a baby," she said.

She was six.

There is not a day when this scene does not come to mind. I see her cropped hair in my memory, under the helmet, lightly shifting as she presses through the turns, grunting against the frame, and holding her balance. She was a different kind of beautiful than she is now. I couldn't see it then. I regret that moment with every spike and crease of my soul.

Then I think of God, walking with me through the courses of my life. The things I try to master—loving my enemies, forgiving those who wrong me, learning to live without anger and lust—and I realize that I am the one being obstinate and losing trust. He sees me, flushed and flustered, and he brings this memory to mind.

I imagine God holding something out to me, something in the shape of a blue bike helmet, and he says, "This belongs to you." It happened. I can't change that now. What I can do is see the grace that it brings when it is new and freshened in the light of God's grace.

I see his gentleness in my abrasiveness. I see his patience in my outburst. I see more in my less.

I truly hate that moment between my daughter and me. I feel it in my bones, whenever the film replays in my head. It belongs to me, however, though we have had beautiful times since. I think more about my words, hearing James's dictum about my tongue being like a spark causing fires (Jas 3:5-6).

My daughter is becoming something entirely different now—something far more complex and brilliant, and my time with the short-haired girl on the bike has closed in a way. I had that moment, that brief shine of sun, and made a choice.

Still, the bike helmet comes to mind and I hear his voice, "This is yours." It can teach me, if I allow that memory a space in my soul. I need to allow the illuminating Spirit that teaches and reminds (Jn 14:17) to give clarity about what has been and create a space in my soul where that hurt might become hopeful.

Every memory belongs.

The spiritual practice of remembering is just that—it is clarity about what *was* so that we can be transformed and engage what *is*.

To remember, then, is an act of redemption; we are bringing to light something from the past and

> *Jesus longs to take our stories and reshape them. The stories and the memories that describe our lives today are the raw material of transformation.*

seeing it as filled with possibility rather than being useless and part of a bygone era. To forget is an act of damnation, condemning and dismissing what has happened before as useless or destructive.

Engaging with our memories is one of the most spiritually courageous things we can do. Seeing the structure our memories have built—the influences and energies—that make us who we are is to enter into the process of unraveling or retelling those stories. It is rewriting the scripts. It is changing things that, though painful, have been our defaults for so long we don't know how to live without them.

It takes courage to let the painful memories of our pasts be redeemed, because we have to learn to live by a different story.

Jesus longs to take our stories and reshape them. The stories and the memories that describe our lives today are the raw material of transformation.

If we dig through all of our memories going backward and arrive at the bedrock, then perhaps we'll find what we've been looking for all along. And we can come forward differently.

The emotions and experiences involved in our implicit memory are things we have gone through. They shape actions we don't even think about any more. The question is: Are we willing to create the space, take the time, and give the energy to explore those emotions and experiences with God so we may become more of the person God created us to be in the first place?

PRACTICE

Making peace with the idea that *every memory belongs* also means getting a grip on the concept that whatever has come before has brought us to where we are, and therefore we must make a place for that reality.

The process of writing a spiritual autobiography can be a helpful practice as we weave together disparate elements of beauty and brutality in our lives. We stop to take an inventory of the larger scenes, where we've been and who we've encountered, and we see the impact of those scenes. If memories write scripts, then our spiritual life has a script that is as vibrant as any Hollywood drama. There are moments of lightness, hilarity, and softness as well as moments of difficulty, failure, and catastrophe.

If every memory belongs, these elements get woven together into a story. When we write our spiritual autobiography, we tend to gravitate to the things that most fit our definition of *spiritual*.

To define *spiritual* from a Christian perspective requires understanding our Christian tradition. Growing up in a Nazarene church, leaning heavily into early twentieth-century holiness movements, the language of salvation from sins by prayer at the altar and the subsequent sanctification were common markers. Acts such as baptism and service fall into this story as well, but ultimately I was given a set of mile markers and metaphors that defined what a spiritual life looked like.

Stop for a moment and think: What are the spiritual milestones of your life? What were your earliest memories of life with God? What moments were given to you, hard-worn by the generations of church folk or family members who went before?

As you write your spiritual autobiography, begin with your earliest memory of interaction with God. Give the details (place, age, and even season) of the event as best as you can.

You will want to include the memory that you brought to the surface in chapter one, as well, as it is part of the bigger picture.

Consider this practice as creating a living document; you will want to add to it over time, specifically as you look for places where God was present or where you did not initially sense his presence in your story.

The hardest work for those of us who have walked significant distances with Jesus is to reevaluate those things that are familiar. The stories are so deeply intertwined, so automatically engaged by our nondeclarative memory that we need a device to step outside our own minds.

For help, you might consider Richard Peace's book *Spiritual Autobiography: Discovering and Sharing Your Spiritual Story* (Colorado Springs: NavPress, 1998).

6

REMEMBERING
WHO WE ARE

Our spiritual lives are where we reckon head-on with the
mystery of ourselves, and the mystery of each other.

Krista Tippett

I walked in 121-degree heat with full confidence of the path
ahead of me. Gathered with other high school students in
Phoenix, Arizona, in 1995, I attended an event called Nazarene
Youth Congress. It was the first time I had ever felt equal levels of
heat from both the pavement and the sun itself. It was the
summer before my senior year of high school, a year that brought
transitions that turned over the soil of my soul and planted seeds
that continue to grow today.

I had already enrolled in college and declared my major as
pre-pharmacy. At the time, I felt it was the best way to make the
most money—a wise way to make long-term decisions, obviously. Never mind that my math and science skills were abysmal.
I joke that in my becoming a pastor and author, and not a phar-
macist, God rescued *thousands*.

What happened in the baking heat of Phoenix, on an evening when I felt God's presence and felt something new arising in me, shifted my story. I heard, not audibly but in the rhythm of my own heart, God bringing to the surface an essential inner truth. I embraced that my skills and energies, and even my gladness, were oriented toward pastoral ministry.

I formed a new plan. I would spend my life as a senior pastor in a Nazarene church in my home state of West Virginia. I would preach, I would "run a church" (whatever that meant) in the way I had seen throughout my churchgoing life. I had the plan and began shaping my life around that plan—from my college choice to books I read to conversations that I began to give greater attention to. Arizona gave me a memory, and I crafted it into a story and a script.

In the world of storytelling, this is called an origin story. An origin story collects memories and stories that inform us of the script a character brings to every action and interaction. Phoenix was a beginning—though not *the* beginning—of what brought me to where I am today.

What I would later learn about this story is echoed by the writer Lee Eisenberg: Some of our stories—our "personal myths"—are founded on faulty information.[1] They come from shells misinterpreted either by our own way of encountering them or by the culture that handed them down to us.

I still believe in the Phoenix story, but the movements of the plot were far more diverse than I had expected.

As you read this, what memories would you say form your origin story? What are the things that brought you to the place where you are? Is it possible that there may be a twist in the plot of that story?

THE MAKING OF A HERO

The story of Exodus is an origin story as well, perhaps the most significant in the Old Testament and in the shaping story of the Jewish people. Exodus begins by gathering the memories, stories, and scripts of a man named Moses.

This is a liberation story, both of a person and of a people.

It begins with his birth in hostile circumstances and then floating down the river in a pitch-coated basket as an infant. In the next glimpse we see, Moses has been told a story about who he is—a refugee from death, a Hebrew but an Egyptian, living in the house of Pharaoh but raised by Hebrews. He has a story about who he is, which is important. Without that story the spiritual work God would do next would be lost.

A moment arises when an injustice is made clear to Moses. This moment reveals something deep within Moses. "One day, after Moses had grown up, he went out to his people and saw their forced labor. He saw an Egyptian beating a Hebrew, one of his kinsfolk. He looked this way and that, and seeing no one he killed the Egyptian and hid him in the sand" (Ex 2:11-12).

In any story, there is a moment when things cannot go back to being the same. Whatever existence Moses had crafted to that point, whatever story and script flowed freely through his daily details, it all shifted. His rage creates a breaking point. This is the point of conflict, tension, and it introduces a new wrinkle into the narrative.

Likely, Moses' life had been moving along a trajectory he had chosen in order to process reality. Joseph Hallinan describes the subliminal reasons behind our responses:

> We create, in short, our own cover stories. These then serve
> as a kind of lens through which we filter our experience of
> the world. They may produce a distorted sense of reality,
> but that distortion can serve a vital function, often by
> making the world appear to be a rational, predictable place
> that we can control.[2]

In other words, Moses had a manageable view of himself that he
could live by. The issue arose quickly—something else was
lurking below the surface.

These moments in life are not simply situations. They are *revelations*. What do you see when you look back at your memories
of impulsiveness, the times when you acted almost automatically
in a way that, up to that point, was unfamiliar or unlikely for you?

Return to that moment now, as I imagine Moses did from
time to time as the Hebrews wandered through the wilderness
toward Canaan. What do you see that surprises you? How has
that moment reverberated through your life and into the present?

We must remember that this story is being told later, *much
later*, almost like the tales of a grandfather sitting on the porch
and drinking tea. I imagine my great-grandfather smoking his
pipe with cherry-flavored tobacco and telling stories of days
gone by. The smell memory is not lost on me, truly.

The stories we tell hold a past reality as *valuable*—valuable
enough to never forget, and instead we pass it on from generation to generation. Regardless of whether those shells are light
and lovely or hard and haggard, they are worth passing on and,
in this case, they are part of the story of a man emerging in relationship with God.

Telling a story of liberation that begins with hot-headed homicide means that memories are not always heroic. In my experience, this is often where transformation begins: in tears, in a cell, in crisis. These are vulnerable memories.

FROM WEAKNESS TO WILDERNESS

Brené Brown says that throughout history, every act of courage began with an act of great vulnerability.[3] To step out, to lead in an intense and difficult time, is not simply about the guts that it takes to move forward. The courage comes from a place of acknowledging that while failure is not an option, it is, in fact, part of our makeup and presence. For us to live any other way is bluster and posturing.

Finding courage through vulnerability means sifting through our shells. The fragments of the life we have lived are stitched together in our memories to form the story of who we are and the script of how we live. The practice of remembering is finding courage for the moment in front of us through confessing the significant personal struggles within and behind us.

Bringing those encoded moments from our memory, the vulnerable moments where our essence has been called out in the open in front of God and everyone, is the root of finding out who we are and what we are given to do.

The narrative of Exodus takes a turn at the death of the slave driver—the

> *To step out, to lead in an intense and difficult time, is not simply about the guts that it takes to move forward. The courage comes from a place of acknowledging that while failure is not an option, it is, in fact, part of our makeup and presence.*

revelation of Moses' inner anger and violence makes him a fugitive from his Egyptian family. I wonder, did he know the Egyptian soldier that he beat to death? Having been raised in the house of Pharaoh, did Moses have a relationship with this soldier who brutalized Moses' Hebrew family?

Then, in a surprise twist, Moses finds that his murder of the oppressor also puts him at odds with the *oppressed*.

> When he went out the next day, he saw two Hebrews fighting; and he said to the one who was in the wrong, "Why do you strike your fellow Hebrew?" He answered, "Who made you a ruler and judge over us? Do you mean to kill me as you killed the Egyptian?" Then Moses was afraid and thought, "Surely the thing is known." When Pharaoh heard of it, he sought to kill Moses.
>
> But Moses fled from Pharaoh. (Ex 2:13-15)

Moses realizes nothing can be the same—his safety, place, and role are being torn away. He is vulnerable, exposed, and off-balance. The safety of Pharaoh's house is gone, and his biological extended family sees him as a threat. In response, he runs to the wilderness. He runs to a place where he has no memories, where his weakness could hide for a while.

If we take a moment to consider our own journeys, we may find times when, regardless of our proximity to spiritual health and growth, the edges of our strength were fading. We were exposed, vulnerable, and the default stories we had trusted disappeared.

Perhaps they are moments of correction—like Jesus calling out his disciples (Mt 17:17) or Nathan incisively whispering, "You are the man" (2 Sam 12:7) at the end of a parable bringing David's adultery and murder to light. Perhaps they are simply the fruit of healthy growth in the grace and knowledge of Jesus (2 Pet 3:18). Each moment takes on a different language, but the effect is largely the same:

You're fired.

I'm leaving.

My faith is changing and I don't know what's next.

We are left vulnerable, open, and off balance. In these moments we are often called to move in a direction we had not planned on. A plot twist rises, so to speak.

YOU AREN'T THE GUY

Nearly twenty years after the Arizona desert, I found myself in a leadership team meeting at the church where I was serving in the Chicago suburbs. After finishing seminary and serving a rural Illinois church, I had moved to Chicagoland and spent eight years on staff as spiritual formation pastor.

Already my origin story had shifted: from senior pastor to associate, from Nazarene to independent Christian church, and from West Virginia to Illinois. If we linger with our memories long enough, we will find that our stories don't always follow the line we had plotted.

I sat surrounded by people I love and had served alongside for years. I had asked for the meeting because of a stirring. I felt drawn to have more of a presence in the weekend teaching schedule, and I had asked for time to gain wisdom from my fellow staff on whether this was a role they could see for me.

We went around the table, and in grace and compassion everyone there said, "We love you and what you do, but we don't feel like you're the guy for that role." I would love to say I received this and simply moved on, but despite the beautiful tension of the meeting, part of me—the Arizona part of me—felt like it was fading.

Who am I? Who am I supposed to be now?

I was also approaching forty, so my thoughts and memories turned to *What do I want to give this part—the most significant part (so to speak)—of my life to? If it isn't this thing that gives me life, then what will it be?* Some part of me wondered if it would be better to never have known at all, never to have risked or put myself in that position of vulnerability.

Yet there are times, whether we are seeking wisdom in our vocation or standing up for injustice, when we need to pick up a vulnerable memory and carry it with us into the next chapter of our story.

That conversation moved me into the wilderness. It moved me into a place of vulnerability where I began to ask new questions about what is most important and what my vocation might be in this next chapter. And I continued to ask, *Who am I now?*

AN EGYPTIAN?

Moses' journey moves to collecting shells in a place called Midian, and one day he has an opportunity to again stand for injustice. A group of women, the daughters of a local priest, are being harassed at a well by other shepherds. Moses protects the women, and that creates an interesting moment when the daughters inform their father, "An Egyptian helped us against the shepherds; he even drew water for us and watered the flock" (Ex 2:19). He is so effective that he actually marries one of the Midianite priest's daughters.

In the wilderness it is possible for our identity to become scuttled and confused. With the typical trappings, goals, and boundaries of our story torn down, we begin to inhabit a variety of different selves. Who are you, Moses? Are you an Egyptian or a Hebrew? Are you a protector or a murderer?

The movement of our spiritual life from growth stage to growth stage constantly strips away the "false self." Robert Mulholland calls the false self it our "self-referenced being"—a being that is strange and awkward compared to our Christ-referenced being, the delightful being we bear at the core of our neurons, blood vessels, muscles, hopes, and dreams. It is "a self that in some way is playing god in its life and in its world."[4]

The false self often takes shape from our memories, stories, and scripts. If we were raised to "never let them see you sweat," then we will portray an unflappable hero to those around us. The false self often leads us to live by forgery, faking a life that we cannot own—a life that simply isn't *ours*.

The false self can also be cast as a hero when we chase what we "believe" God desires of us. While this can incorporate forgery just as well, it can also simply be the self that exists for a period of time and then needs to be shed in order to move to the next stage of life. We may read this statement and nod, but our memories are dogged and do not relent easily. Sue Monk Kidd says,

> As we attempt to adapt to and protect ourselves from the wounds and realities of life, we each create a unique variety of defense structures—patterns of thinking, behaving and relating designed to protect the ego. These egocentric patterns make up our false selves. . . . The spiritual journey

entails confronting these hardened patterns that we've spent a lifetime creating, patterns that oppose the life of the spirit and obscure our true spiritual identity.[5]

Moses is the Hebrew-Egyptian who is now wanted by his Egyptian family and scorned by his Hebrew family. And he carves a new identity as the Egyptian shepherd married to the daughter of the priest of Midian. In the midst of the wilderness, various *selves* fly through Moses' field of vision. How does God settle this? How do we move through these selves?

It is our journey from pretending that we have no doubts about God to embracing the memories of tear-stained pillows and abandoned quiet time. It is the journey from needing the *feeling of God* that we remember from our early walk with Jesus to feeling the *need for God* for his own sake.

If we are to engage our memories for the sake of our formation through Jesus, we will be active in finding the memories, stories, and scripts that have given shape to our current self. It may be a self that we need to lose in order to find the one God has designed for us (Mt 16:25).

The purpose of the wilderness is to strip clean our stories and scripts of the false self. God is doing purifying work on Moses (and on us). This moment creates an important memory for Moses, as he will return to this same wilderness later in the story. For now, and for us, the wilderness is a place where God often brings us to encounter the false self of our stories so we might find something all the more powerful.

Which brings us to an encounter with a bush that will not burn up.

A FIRE IN THE WILDERNESS

In the summer of 2016, just a few weeks after my conversation with our leadership team, I was offered a seven-week sabbatical. It was timely for many reasons: I had finished my first book manuscript and was coming to a place of physical and spiritual exhaustion. The summer would be filled with travel and family, reading, and hopefully rest.

During that summer, a door opened for me to consider a role at another church that included teaching and preaching. I looked at the description and said, "This is who I am. This is the best fit," and my wife concurred.

We talked to people we considered to be wise counselors, we prayed, we thought and processed with family, and by summer's end we began to entertain the idea of leaving our home and community of nearly eight years to move into a new role.

In my memory of that moment, I see that God often meets us in the wilderness with clarity and brilliance. He meets us when we are most vulnerable and engages us at the level of what we need. Or in this case, what we *believe* we need.

Within three months we had sold our house and moved to Rockford, Illinois, where I took on the role of teaching pastor. As we unpacked boxes in a new place, which of course included a new school and new neighbors, something seemed disjointed. The memory of standing in the midst of the move-in chaos is fresh in my mind. A story was emerging.

A story emerges for Moses as well. As he watches the sheep, Moses is confronted by a light glinting above the ridge that throws shadows on the pastureland ahead. He spots a bush alight with flame, but not consumed. He hears a voice and is welcomed to holy ground, provided he leave behind the dirt and accumulated sheep pellets of his sandals. Then, a voice directs, "The cry of the Israelites has now come to me; I have also seen how the Egyptians oppress them. So come, I will send you to Pharaoh to bring my people, the Israelites, out of Egypt" (Ex 3:9-10).

Moses takes a shell in his hand, the experience of God speaking and giving an unreasonable and impossible mission. It would remain with him until his head, weary with age, would fall to the darkness. The murderer, scorned by both his adopted family of slave owners and his genetic family of slaves, must turn on the one and win over the other.

Could it be any other way?

Freedom begins when God finds us in the midst of normalcy and orients our vision toward a fracture, a crack in the beauty that needs our attention. Spiritual formation is the understanding that we are both invited to seal that fracture in our own life as well as tending to the brokenness of systems and individuals around us. Yet it will not begin in earnest for us—or for Moses—until the depths of our false self are drawn into the light.

A burning bush is a more than adequate source of that kind of light.

Burning-bush moments often happen in the wilderness. God meets us in dark spaces, transitional spaces, vulnerable spaces where we feel like tourists stranded in our own lives and are unable to speak or understand the language. They are memories

> *Freedom begins when God finds us in the midst of normalcy and orients our vision toward a fracture, a crack in the beauty that needs our attention.*

that dot our everyday encounters with God, bringing energy and clarity when we desperately need it.

Yet the burning bush has a secondary function as well; it serves as a mirror in which we see who we really are. The burning bush reveals our true self, and that experience creates a memory that invites us to move toward a new story. We write a new script.

Our true self flourishes in beauty, goodness, and truth—in the ways God has uniquely crafted us. It is the outflow of what St. Irenaeus describes as "man fully alive." It is that deep gift we have to give to the world, knitted by our experiences, clarified by our memories and stories, and executed by the resulting script.

If you had asked me, standing among the boxes in Rockford, what the burning-bush moment was in this entire story, I would have said the sabbatical time. With the gift of memory and the privilege of engaging with God in this last year, I now see things differently.

From time to time, I read the words of Parker Palmer to remind me of the realities of the burning bush in my own life: "Vocation does not come from a voice 'out there' calling me to become something I am not. It comes from a voice 'in here' calling me to be the person I was born to be, to fulfill the original selfhood given me at birth."[6]

Moses is called to a vocation at the burning bush, but it is not something outside of his experience or memory. It is the reality of injustice at the sight of an Egyptian beating his enslaved brother, to which he responded aggressively. As Ruth Haley Barton says so well, "It was becoming clear that his calling was inextricably interwoven with his human situation and his personal history. . . . Even though his violent reaction to the injustice that he witnessed had been terribly wrong, the incident itself was not irrelevant. It arose from something real within."[7]

Moses' story, built on memories and experiences long past, had been massively reinterpreted by this new fire rising from within. In a surprising twist, that fire was the light in the wilderness. It was the vocation he never knew he had, rising from the emotions and experiences that went before.

No doubt, he had to discard the old story of living forever as a fugitive shepherd in the wilderness. He had to lay down the old story of living in Pharaoh's house and dining in the safety of empire. He had to embrace a new shell, a new story, and a future filled with miracles and massacre that would set a nation free.

I went to Rockford believing that I was going to live out the true self that the "fire" of conversation and sabbatical had set alight. Instead, I went to Rockford and had a true burning-bush moment there. Everything that came before was merely a match struck in the dark.

The true self is not easily embraced or discovered. The Spirit of Jesus leans into us, discerning our hearts where our will and desire play (Mt 9:4), but we are often the last to listen to the rumblings rising from within.

THE WIND BLOWS WHERE IT WILL

My wife and I walked a paved trail around the local YMCA in Rockford. It was a familiar walk, but in my memory this walk had a burning-bush significance. My wife had been offered an expanded position with her company, one that would require her to work out of the office near our old Chicagoland home. The commute from Rockford was not feasible, so a move would be required.

We looked at each other and agreed: "It may be time to move on."

In that year, a new vocation rose both from within and without. I had signed a contract for the book you are reading, and writing was coming to life in a way that it had not in the past. The person who emerged from the Nazarene Youth Congress in 1995 didn't say anything about writing.

I'm sure the Moses living in Pharaoh's house never considered being a liberator, either.

In the wind-swept fields beyond the YMCA, we came to terms with taking whatever step it took to pursue the movement toward writing and a new role for my wife. We would learn that a part-time position was possible at my previous church, though we would have to rethink our financial situation.

In due time, nearly eighteen months after the summer sabbatical, we found ourselves back in familiar neighborhoods and schools. While it was a homecoming of sorts, what strikes me now is the memory of how buying and selling two houses and moving my daughter through four schools in two years began to put to death a false self that had gone well past its time.

Writer Heather Kopp talks about the moment she left rehab and headed home, prepared to engage life apart from alcohol. She says, "The most amazing thing about being an alcoholic or addict who suddenly gets sober is that from now on the time line of your life will always have a thick black line separating everything before you quit from everything that comes next. But when you're standing with your back up against that black line, you wonder how on earth you can possibly go forward."[8]

Freedom from a false self that is woven tightly into our memories, stories, and scripts isn't going to come easily. As Kopp says, any time we cut a new path in our journey of transformation, there is a moment of no return that causes us to tremble. We hesitate in this true self, we are reluctant, and we second-guess whether our move into the unknown could possibly be a move in step with God.

We feel this way for good reason too.

Moving my family did not come without pain and disappointment. For a time I second-guessed my decision, but the deeper we went into our return to "home" I doubted it less. My wife reminded me during a long car ride of my hesitancy. There will always be a nervous step when moving closer to the true self, because the shells we've gathered suggest authenticity is somehow dangerous.

I have memories of my own wisdom and haste in moving, memories I am still processing and learning from in this new stage. Would I be able to pursue writing with the skill and ability necessary now that it had moved from the periphery to the center of my focus? For these memories to be fruitful, I need to see them as light instead of darkness because that is what they have become.

For some, the happily-ever-after story will not emerge. God will awaken our senses to a new direction, we will choose it, and struggles will compound like April rains. It is important to remember that the narratives of real life are rarely black and white. While the Hebrew slaves celebrated their newfound freedom, the Egyptians mourned the deaths of their firstborn (Ex 12:29-30).

Moses expresses a great deal of reluctance in his new vocation: from struggles with speech and authority to a simple unwillingness to be the one to carry the liberator's staff. Perhaps he was content in the wilderness. It is easy to stay in the point between false and true self if we so choose.

As someone who has the privilege of leading silent, multiday retreats, I am often asked, "Why can't we stay here?" I can relate: we could remain in the quiet spaces, taking walks through nature and sipping hot tea on wind-blown afternoons, centering ourselves in that quiet space in our hearts where we meet Jesus in all of his compassion and grace. That is not, however, where the fullness of our life is lived.

We cannot remain forever in the present, pushing pause on the collection of new shells to simply gaze at the ones we already have.

The true self is always a gift not only to our own selves, fortified and growing in the love and likeness of Jesus, but also to the greater community of humanity. Frederick Buechner puts it this way: "The place God calls you to is the place where your deep gladness and the world's deep hunger meet."[9]

Our time in the wilderness, experiencing God's compassionate revelation of our true self, is never meant to be hoarded but to be shared. Our true self is a gift to be shared, a story to be told, and a script that makes light the hearts and lives of others.

A LIVING REMINDER

Moses embraces his true self and leads the Hebrews—now called Israel—out of slavery. His liberated, true self becomes the liberation of a nation weighted by slavery.

They wobble through the Red Sea on dry land and enter a wilderness that looked familiar to Moses. He remembers watching sheep in these scrublands and ultimately encountering the God who knew him beyond the false self.

The liberation of Israel and the liberation of Moses intersect on *terra firma* (solid ground). In that moment, with Israel stripped of familiarity and completely dependent on his generosity, God offers a gift: "The LORD has given you the sabbath, therefore on the sixth day he gives you food for two days; each of you stay where you are; do not leave your place on the seventh day" (Ex 16:29).

Sabbath rest is the healthy act of moving from the false self created by our various slaveries and toward the true self of work that flows from a far richer source.

Is it any wonder that one of the prominent commandments is, "Remember the sabbath day, and keep it holy" (Ex 20:8)?

Sabbath rest for the Hebrews was an act of performance art that forever remained linked to a historical reality, a deep and reenacted kind of memory that wore grooves in their synaptic connections.

In effect it says, "You are free people, and the new world you will live in is a world where you will work to sustain life rather than to *create* life. In other words, your creativity will be in service to the initial Creator—the first—and therefore Sabbath is a day for you to simply *remember* that control of the universe (even your small acreage thereof) is beyond your pay grade."

The false self says that effort equals identity.

The true self says, "I am free to live gracefully and freely with Jesus because my identity has already been given and my work is simply a response to my identity."

Sabbath is the art of remembering the distance created by the false self and releasing it at the most basic level, where we believe we are in control of the world. The first formal practice outside of Egypt is the specific act of asking the false self to come to the foreground. Busyness, activity, and productivity are delicate traps calling us to break a vow so we feel better about our use of time.

As it happens, the true self lives with more fervor when we reenact and remember a story that puts the false self to death on a weekly basis.

PRACTICE

After reading about the true and false self, it may make sense to take some time to rest with these concepts, to let them sink in.

Mark Buchanan's words on sabbath are helpful:

> The Exodus command, with its call to imitation, plays on a hidden irony: we mimic God in order to remember we're not God. In fact, that is a good definition of Sabbath: *imitating God so that we stop trying to be God.* We mirror divine behavior only to freshly discover our human limitations. Sabbath-keeping involves a recognition of our own weakness and smallness, that we are made from dust, that we hold our treasure in clay jars, and that without proper care we break.[10]

A sabbath rest is when we disconnect from our normal rhythms of personal productivity in order to remember that it is God who creates, sustains, and enlivens us. Obviously, Jesus took liberties with sabbath rest (Mt 12:1-8), but in the end he echoed God's gift of sabbath by giving it back to us in grace to benefit our lives (Ex 16:29).

As a guide for this practice, we want to focus on specific memories that are relevant to the true and false self discussion. Perhaps the memory you chose early in the book will work here. If not, choose another burning-bush memory to keep in mind during your time of sabbath rest.

- First, choose a significant period of time when you can clear out your calendar. While four to eight hours is ideal, one to two hours will work as well. (Practicing sabbath rest typically creates a hunger for more.)
- Plan this time with those you share life with—family, roommates, parents. It is best to plan a time of sabbath rest in advance so you

can limit the number of distractions and other variables. Practicing sabbath rest as a group requires more coordination (saying no to sports or other activities that would interfere with the rest period).

- Decide what the time will look like in advance. Set an "out of office" response on your email. Put your phone on "Do Not Disturb" or airplane mode. I suggest as much time as possible for quiet reflection, engagement with nature, or even sleep. Try not to create another to-do list that is simply the sabbath version of your typical day.

- Do things that give you life. While it is best to restrict technology (if not cut it out entirely) during sabbath rest, you may want to watch a movie that gives you great joy. If coloring, working on puzzles, or even gardening gives you energy, then plan to make those activities part of sabbath rest. The important guiding principle is to limit activities to those things that have no real productive outcome other than sheer enjoyment and reenergizing your spirit.

- In light of our memory discussion, make a point to return to a phrase such as "Today I rest as a way of remembering the God who created, loves, and cares for my true self." If you can, commit this to memory and repeat it throughout the rest time, or simply write it down where you can return to it often.

- If possible, close the time with a meal or time of prayer that marks the movement from rest to work. Take a moment to reflect on the sabbath rest period and make a note of significant things you remember from the time of rest. Write these down so you can refer to them through the coming week.

7

COMING BACK AGAIN

Forgetfulness leads to exile. Remembrance is the secret of redemption.

BAAL SHEM TOV

*I*n the film *Memento*, we meet Leonard, who is searching for the man who killed his wife.[1] He appears to be the typical Hollywood hero of the early 2000s. The hair is right; the jaw line, the atmosphere, everything screams revenge film. However, Christopher Nolan's movie has a significant twist: Leonard has no short-term memory. He can remember life before his wife died, but anything since drifts from his recollection in a matter of minutes.

As the movie progresses, we find that Leonard has an intricate system of tattoos with clues he does not want to forget. He creates Post-it notes detailing dates and events, plus he has a dubious friend who is "helping" him with his mission.

We watch him stumble into situation after situation and try to figure out what is going on as if he has been dropped into the moment from outside of time itself. Of course, this is what happens when we lose our short-term memory. Every moment becomes disoriented, disconnected from a larger story, in other words, terrifying.

The film ends, strangely, at the beginning. While I won't ruin the plot, I will say that everything you see in the film has already happened. Without a short-term memory, life goes in reverse, with each moment trailing the one before, and Leonard never realizes that everywhere he goes is a place he has been before. How could he?

We are no different. In our journey of remembering our lives gone by, we realize there are many places we come to and know as places where we've been before.

As I read my journals of the last year, I highlighted words that are repeated: words like *discipline*, *rhythms*, *contentment*, and *peace*. The challenges I face today seem familiar because the yellow-tinted words in my journal tell me, "I have been here before."

Where do you find yourself today, in your journey with Jesus, that is clearly a return trip? Would you rather be somewhere else?

In commenting on the movie *Memento*, Glenn Paauw says, "Mementos can only do so much. They function best as symbols or stand-ins. . . . Alone and out of context, they can easily fail to do their job. . . . His mementos give him slices of a story, but not the real thing."[2]

And when we look at the story of Scripture, specifically the life of Moses in the book of Deuteronomy, we learn that when all we have are isolated memories, we lose one of God's greatest gifts to us: wisdom.

THE FIRST TIME AROUND

In the story of Israel walking toward the Promised Land and living into their newly minted liberation, there is a dark spot. Confronted with all they had been promised only to see that it came at a cost—the cost of their own true fears and hesitations—

they pause. In that pause comes doubt and finally the abandonment of their destination (Num 13:25-33).

The failure makes no sense whatsoever to a modern reader.

In the story of the exodus we see the continual illustration of God's presence and provision. Surely these wandering, liberated men and women could recall the manna, the quail, the water blasting forth out of dry stone.

We are not so different. We face the challenge of a difficult circumstance, one where we are asked to step out of our own sense of ability and confidence, and we pause. We doubt. Our memories have created deep and rich chapters in our story. We have a script that reveals where we move in moments like these. And yet, with all the evidence in the world, we pause.

Remember, our formation journey is rarely linear and *never* perfect. We grasp grace by realizing that we are obedient and obstinate, often both within a single moment. The people who left Egypt under the cover of darkness, walked through an open window in the water, and ate from the hand of God himself suddenly experience spiritual amnesia.

As Leighton Ford eloquently puts it, "In a very real sense we humans are spiritual amnesiacs, trying to remember who we are, where we came from, and where we must go to come home to our hearts."[3] Even with the taste of fire-warmed unleavened bread lingering on their tongues, the Hebrews had forgotten where (and in whom) home could be found. And we are no different.

The destructive quality of spiritual amnesia is that we forget the *promise* in the light of the *problem*, and we also forget the times when the *provision* was made for us and we found ourselves standing safe and secure on the other side.

The Hebrews lose track of their shells. They dismantle the memories, silence their stories, and set the script ablaze. As a result, they are given forty years of wandering and meandering to contemplate what has happened (Num 14:20-24).

Israel's journey in the desert is an apt metaphor for our own journey through failure, shortsightedness, or ignorance. This wilderness haunts us. It enhances and draws to the surface memories we'd rather forget, stories we're all too familiar with, scripts that appear inevitable. Our shells of provision are replaced with the shells of panic.

Neurologically this makes sense. The emotionally charged experiences of anxiety, fear, and panic bypass our typical memory-processing center (the hippocampus) and move straight to long-term memory through the amygdala, where our fight-or-flight response is housed.[4] It is hard to shake the emotional impact something of scarcity.

The story of the exodus helps us see the wilderness journey of Moses from his false self to his true self and invites us to chart our own memories accordingly. The story of failure in Deuteronomy is just as valuable. Every memory belongs. The same is true for us.

Deuteronomy's narrative is about Moses bringing the people *back*. They are the descendants of the original crew who stood in panic at the sight of Canaan. They look like their grandparents and parents, with the same eyes and same idiosyncrasies.

TRY, TRY AGAIN

With a title like "Deuteronomy" it is difficult to fly under the radar. Biblical word play begs us to take notice. Two Greek words, *deutero*, which means "second," and *nomos*, which means "law," set up an interesting concept.

However, the book is not about a distinct and separate set of instructions (laws). Moses, the leader and lawgiver of the book of Exodus, also gives the instruction in Deuteronomy. It is not a change, however. Far from it. It is instead both a *return* and a *redirection*.

It is a reminder: "Let's look at the shells again. Let us see them for what they are. Then let's embrace them and find our place in light of them."

Return might be a hard word because an entire generation of desert wanderers has died since their escape from Egypt. The books of Leviticus and Numbers chronicle the journey, disobedience, deception, and pain of the wilderness, but in Deuteronomy the story takes a sharp turn.

Family members who sat by the fire telling stories of what it was like to be in Egypt are now long gone. Children have become parents and even grandparents in the period between then and the moment the people of promise left the people of pain. "These are the words that Moses spoke to all Israel beyond the Jordan— in the wilderness" (Deut 1:1).

"Beyond the Jordan" is poetry to the ears of the wilderness walkers. It is the destination their forefathers and foremothers longed for, prayed for, fought for, and suffered for. The day has come; the journey is nearly over.

When we follow God into our memories to revisit our stories and revise our scripts, there are as many moments of anticipation of a journey well-walked as there are moments of grinding our teeth in the night.

When we look back on our life and we begin to see that God has been shaping us through a long-term project, a move, or a particular moment, it is easier to see the full movement on display. We take little scenes and weave them together to understand the bigger story.

That is Israel's story. That is our story.

When we first got married my wife and I were filled with bluster and insecurity, but now we have found comfort with each other. We have come to know the depths of each other so that we can engage with a love beyond romantic notions. We have come to the place where love is not an emotion per se but a choice made daily that ignites our commitment and engagement with each other. In a marriage, a friendship, or even a profession, we go from being new and fresh to where we commit daily to the work ahead of us. All of these movements illustrate history in motion and transition.

> *A life of grace is not perfect, because the presence of grace requires the relative absence of perfection.*

In our honest moments, we want the process of spiritual formation to end at some point. I want to become perfect, whole, patient, graceful, and generous without hesitation, and I would like to see that reality come in my lifetime. We wander through Google trying to find disciplines, studies, and experiences that might facilitate the deep magic that turns our tumblers and unlocks the bonds that keep us from a life of perfection.

Perfection is too much.

Grace is enough.

A life of grace is not perfect because the presence of grace requires the relative absence of perfection.

Grace is what has brought the Hebrew people to the Jordan. Grace delivered them from the fate their ancestors faced after disobedience and disgrace. They are at the same place, and they are confronted with the memory of a great failure.

Grace is a hard thing to remember, mainly because the place where we need it most is often the moment we are furthest from our understanding of it. Peter extends the invitation to "grow in the grace and knowledge of our Lord and Savior Jesus Christ" (2 Pet 3:18). To grow is to return to grace and feel its subtle but beautiful wisdom.

Regardless of our hopes, spiritual formation will require us to process our greatest failures. This isn't some morbid requirement; it is quite frankly the only way we move toward wisdom. Without grace, our failures cannot become wisdom.

The story of Deuteronomy gives us the challenge of returning to the memory of failure. The return to the boundary of Canaan means that Canaan—the promise, the life that was beyond life— had been left behind before. To return is an acknowledgement: we wandered away and now we return the same but different.

For Moses to come back to this place is the same as us coming to the table with a jagged shell.

THE WISDOM OF THE SECOND COAT

We recently moved into a new house, and I spent the majority of our first week painting. Seven out of the nine rooms, some of them getting two coats, took on new colors to embrace their new inhabitants.

With that much painting, I learned a few things. I learned that speed is not my friend. I learned that "I'll just avoid that spot when I get there" are famous last words, and there *will* be red paint on the white ceiling. Count on it.

The most significant thing I learned was that the best way to atone for mistakes of a first coat is *another* coat. Granted, it's possible to repeat the same missteps the second time around, but at least on the second run we can *see* the issues and address them. This is what wisdom is—wisdom is seeing the first coat and dealing with it via the second coat. It is a way of engaging memories that says, "I've been here before."

When we travel, we consult those who have already made the same journey. We need to know what to expect.

Tradespeople enter into a relationship of *apprenticeship*, learning from those who have snipped wires and secured welds in the past so they might learn what to do and more importantly what not to do.

The benefit of our returning to the same place—our memories, stories, and scripts—is that we see it again, but different from the first time, with the benefit of wandering in the interim. The memory viewed with distance changes us, and we learn what it means to receive the moment with gratitude and act in the light of what God's gracious spirit has already taught us. Our neurological profile has changed, and we have created synaptic connections for both the failure and the freedom, the wandering and coming home. A return then is both familiar and new to our moldable minds.

Grace, then, often multiplies as we recall our larger story with God.

I often have conversations with people in spiritual crisis who talk about feeling distant from God. The challenge of the distance of God is that we see it as a problem to be solved. I typically ask this question in those scenarios: "When was the last time you felt God's presence?" I welcome them back to a place, a season, a situation. Perhaps it would be helpful to do that now: When was the last time you felt God's presence—intimate, gracious, and sustaining?

I appeal to a memory in those moments, and Deuteronomy does the same. The memory of Moses helps us understand that though God appears distant to us, *there is wisdom in the wandering.*

NOTHING NEW TO OLD EYES

The spiritual journey with Jesus has happened before.

Christian spiritual formation has a deep and rich history— saints and ramblers who have gone before and created a litany of reflections that give light and depth to the challenges we face today. It is no mistake that many of the ancient voices in the formation journey—those my friend J. K. Jones refers to as the "dead guys" (gender neutral, of course)—are called spiritual fathers and mothers.[5]

Deuteronomy carries a beautiful command that is the heart of Moses. When talking about the laws of the land they are about to enter, Moses says, "Teach them to your children, talking about them when you are at home and when you are away, when you lie down and when you rise" (Deut 11:19). Our literal fathers and mothers, as well as the spiritual fathers and mothers, are part of our journey toward wisdom.

Some of the most interesting conversations I have with my daughter are about my life when I was her age. She laughs at my childhood fears, not in jest but with incredulity that her dad ever feared anything. That hallway. The one between the bathroom and my parents' room. (She snickers.)

We talk about my wandering life as a Christian teenager, leveraging a spiritual life and consistent church attendance into a fairly active dating résumé. We talk about Holley and me in our early life and marriage, newly minted adults screaming and throwing things while our best friend stood by the screen door waiting for a quiet moment to ask, "Can I come in now?"

During these tours of my life, I often say to my daughter, "There was a time when I was not a very good person." I say it with my whole heart. I hurt people close to me, sometimes intentionally. I took advantage of my influence as a popular person in my school. I abused my relationships with friends and girlfriends. My overall motivations were self-centered and self-motivated.

I am a courier of my memories, relaying them to my daughter and engaging with them in front of her. Why in the world would I be so transparent and direct with my daughter? Or in the case of Moses, why would he have such strong emotions about the past?

The answer is simple. I have tried, perhaps because I am an interior person and enjoy these flights of historical navel gazing, to allow Jesus to walk in and around my story and reveal it for what it is. Then, I go to where my daughter is and return with her again. The moment is hers now, her chance to decide, to relate, to engage.

What I offer her is wisdom. Memories are the raw material that God can shape into wisdom if we engage our wandering ways with him.

LEARNING FROM THE DARK

The journey of formation has led me to understand not only the past darkness of my life but also the wisdom that has exploded through the bleak depths of memory like a diamond sparkling in the sun. I turn this diamond in the light, and every time I tell the story of failure and faltering, I give a gift of wisdom to my daughter. She will fail on her own, but she should never fail in my steps.

Wisdom informs us that much is the same from generation to generation. Life as it is, in this skin and in this place, has not undergone a metamorphosis. What is good for you now will carry your children forward into the future. Give them shells, help them remember.

Eric Kandel says, "Memory is essential not only for the continuity of individual identity, but also for the transmission of culture and for the evolution and continuity of societies over centuries. . . . All human accomplishments, from antiquity to modern times, are products of a shared memory accumulated over centuries, whether through written records or through a carefully protected oral tradition."[6]

The teacher of Ecclesiastes cries, "There is nothing new under the sun" (Eccles 1:9). But wisdom tells us there are many things that are *old* under this aching sun, and there is much to learn from those old things.

Moses, for example, is forty years older when he stands before the Hebrews beyond the Jordan than when he stood before the flaming bush and saw his true self for the first time.

Nothing is new under the sun. We've been here before, but we are wizened and weathered. So let's teach our kids about the sun itself; take that formation and give it away. Wisdom is where memory becomes a *gift*, so much so that to sustain God's people in the Promised Land the gift must be commanded.

People must pass down the old things under this same sun to inform the memories and lives of those who will live out their days underneath it. We hope they live with our wisdom as a guide; we hope they live with more joy and grace, but the sun is the same.

As my daughter begins to find boys, shall we say, *interesting*, I find myself suddenly aware of my own intentions and proclivities as a preteen boy. I see them, the shells collected in those hormone-blighted years, and suddenly I feel like building an iron tower and locking my daughter Rapunzel in it until these savages get control of themselves.

I suppose that is one way of handling things.

Another is to say, "I know the way they walk. There is nothing new under the sun, but I am an *old* teenage boy. I know the way looking backward, so the best I can do is to describe the scenery to my daughter."

I talk to her about what these still-maturing men are thinking, what they hope to accomplish, and why they fall all over themselves with ego and awkwardness in her presence. It is wisdom to say, "I have been here before. I have regrets and failures under this sun that I'd rather not rehash but instead take them and redeem them for your sake. For the sake of others."

Didn't Jesus say, "Wisdom is vindicated by all her children" (Lk 7:35)? If that is the case, then there is something about the Hebrews' experience of wandering the desert that is essential for those yet to come.

There is something essential to you and me as well. It is the value of memories to the formation of wisdom, which Dallas Willard calls "the knowledge of how to live well" following after Jesus.[7]

If wisdom is vindicated by her children, then the story of Moses and Israel hobbling in the wilderness becomes the birthing suite where God plays midwife to the delivery of

Typically, wisdom comes at a cost and through sacrifice.

wisdom to another generation. This is wisdom that comes at a cost and through sacrifice.

Without these memories, however, all of our formation is simply reactionary. We jump to fix a present-tense reality because it is new and strange, as if no one has ever seen it before. My own personal struggle lies here because as a person who identifies as an Enneagram 4, I am constantly overconfident in the uniqueness of my situation.[8]

The writer of Ecclesiastes, however, is the corrective to those identifying as Enneagram 4s: "There is nothing new under the sun." Remember?

We need elders to gift the generation that follows with the details of their failures, reminding us that these things have happened before. Without a Moses with forty years of sand between his toes, or without spiritual fathers and mothers who have walked the journey with Jesus before us, we are left to our own devices and limited sight.

In the embrace of wisdom—especially the wisdom with bruises—we learn the inheritance we have come into. Moses' command to teach the laws must, by necessity, come with the story of disobedience and wandering in the desert. When the wandering eyes and hearts of the children are caught in the gaze of wizened souls, they hear a story that says, "I've been there before. Here is what happened. Watch that you do not find yourself there as well."

WISDOM'S CHOICE

Recently, I talked with a friend named Rich who has spent his working years in the audiovisual world. As we talked about his newest role, he reflected on what it means to be the oldest on his team by twenty-plus years. At his stage of life, he was coming to terms with his true self. "This is who I am. This is who I am not," he quipped. This is the insight of engaging the true self, by the way. It is the wisdom of the wilderness, and typically a gift we receive only when we have whacked our forehead against reality a time or two.

He has found an interesting gift in being the elder statesman on his team.

In a conversation he had with a younger colleague, Rich shared his insight on how to read a client. "You can see how they will treat you," he said, "by the way they treat themselves and others." He counseled his younger colleague to watch carefully and protect himself, especially when the client was antagonistic for no reason.

A follow-up conversation with that same team member proved his wisdom right. A client who acted out negatively in a meeting did the same later in private, only this time the target was Rich's young colleague.

From the labor pains of our memories of failure comes the birth of wisdom that leads us to live well on the journey with Jesus.

Though I didn't press, I knew where this wisdom came from: a painful moment when this same response came crashing down on my friend's head. He had been there. He had done that.

There is nothing new under the sun.

There is something else going on in this story: my friend is redeeming some hard-won, scar-saturated memories, stories, and scripts. The fight that brings us wisdom is one that God often wraps and presents to others as a great act of tying our stories back into the *cantus primus* I mentioned earlier.

Of course, this only makes sense because the spiritual practice of remembering means that every memory belongs: the failures of Israel a generation past, the failures of a teenage boy without understanding or grace, the failure to see an impending betrayal through the clear signals of a client, or the failures of whatever specter of yourself you choose to name and bring forth from within your own story.

From the labor pains of our memories of failure comes the birth of wisdom that leads us to live well on the journey with Jesus.

THE LAST WILL OF WISDOM

Moses comes to a point of surrendering his leadership to the young man Joshua (Deut 31:14-23), reminding us that the fullness of the journey to the true self always ends with some sort of "giving up." When Moses surrenders leadership, he is fighting with his neurological pathways that have been shaped since the burning bush for the work of liberation and leadership. Now he has to trust the wisdom and memories he has shared with Joshua (and all of Israel for that matter).

Wisdom through our memories often means surrendering what used to be poetry to embrace what is now song. Moses moves from liberator to legend. I have moved from being a child to a parent and will one day hopefully embrace the story and script of being a grandparent.

This is why the end of Deuteronomy portrays a timely moment when Moses speaks of *choice*. Living freely with our failures and our hard-won wisdom creates the opportunity to present a choice to ourselves and to others.

One of the most beautiful parts of being a parent or mentoring another leader is the moment when I can say, "What do you think we should do?" Moving to a place where we trust the ability of others to choose wisely ushers them into the memory-making process with God. Moses says, "I have set before you life and death, blessings and curses. Choose life so that you and your descendants may live, loving the LORD your God, obeying him, and holding fast to him; for that means life to you and length of days" (Deut 30:19-20).

In *The Secret Life of the Mind*, Mariano Sigman says we make choices based on a cerebral mechanism that "converts the information it has gathered from the senses into votes for one option or the other. The voices pile up in the form of ionic currents accumulated in a neuron until they reach a threshold where the brain deems there is sufficient evidence."[9]

Moses has provided the information, both what he heard from God and what he experienced with God. With the invitation to Israel to "choose," he is calling their brains to tally the votes.

Our memories are doing the same. The accumulation of shells produces a kind of wisdom in us, that we have been this way before. And now with those shells stacked at our feet, we are invited to choose.

We may choose a new story about our relationships, about race, about our faith.

We may choose to remain steadfast and dedicated to God and others who have proved themselves trustworthy and life-giving.

These choices form us, and each one provides a shell that we collect until one day we retrieve it again to live it out in the breath of the Spirit of God.

THE POWER OF CHOICE

Choice was not part of the equation in the exodus. Choice was not part of Moses' language in the desert. Choice is the playground of wisdom, which is why Jesus never forced anyone to follow him on the journey to becoming who we truly are—the beloved sons and daughters of God.

Choice comes from remembering that there is an option other than Canaan. We can choose our own fear instead of abundance, a life that is only marginally complete. We can choose a life of slavery instead of freedom, and the Hebrews remember that reality because every seventh day they wisely observe sabbath rest and remember what it means to be cared for and free. Slaves are not given the choice of sabbath. What if the true wisdom of our memories is to remind us that choosing any sort of slavery is a choice against the "new creation" we have become (2 Cor 5:17)?

When we fully possess our memories of failure, it allows us to give the gift of life and death. When Moses says, "I have set before you life and death," I have typically read that to mean the laws restated at the verge of their promised context. However, the intention of Deuteronomy—despite the name—is not simply renewed legislation. Moses' life is on display: his courage, his failure, and his vulnerability. Perhaps he is saying, *I embody the life that comes in prayer and trust.*

I know life and death.

I know blessings and curses.

I know how to hold fast to God, and how to let my anger win out over memories of his promises.

Note that for Moses this is the endpoint of an examined journey, and for us these moments come quite often. We have the choice to examine our experiences, memories, stories, and scripts to find the wisdom that grows out of that rich soil.

Moses can say, "I set before you life and death," because he has seen and reflected on both.

Telling the story a second time in Deuteronomy reveals Moses has engaged in significant contemplation. Thomas Merton defines contemplation as "the work of the Holy Ghost acting on our souls through His gifts of Wisdom and understanding with special intensity to increase and perfect our love for Him."[10]

Deuteronomy then becomes not only a call to focus the people on loving God and him alone (Deut 6:4-6). Inherent in the book is a thoughtful reflection on Moses' memories and the resulting way of wisdom that leads away from wandering and into the land that has been promised.

"This is my wisdom," he says. "Here it is, stripped bare, illustrated by my memories that I've given you today as a gift. So choose. Choose to find wisdom in both my memories of wandering and of faithfulness."

Many of us can say that. We have spent nights seeking God for things we don't understand. We have a Bible underlined in pinks and yellows, with notes and exclamation points for transformational moments in our lives. We have journals with notes about silence spent in a prairie field, watching native tallgrass sway, and pondering Jesus' words about the Spirit (Jn 3:8).

We find those memories and know that our life up to this point is made of them.

But Moses is also saying, "I embody the life that comes from disobedience and frustration."

We nod and say amen. We see moments when we refused to forgive, when we loved ourselves so much that our neighbors became expendable. We see moments when we double-checked the locks on our doors because of the skin tone of our neighbors two doors down. We see ourselves allowing fear, smallness, and limited beauty to rule our moments and our days. We know that our life to that moment is built of such shoddy shells. Every memory belongs.

When we have our hands firmly around those times of joy and disappointment, failure and freedom, we can truly say to ourselves and others, "I have the wisdom of both life and death to offer. I've seen it all. Watch me, let me share my story and script with you. Then, choose."

PRACTICE

In this practice we want to revisit the memories, stories, and scripts we've lived with in the last few hours, days, weeks, or months. Similar to Moses' reflections in Deuteronomy, this practice is a way of seeing your life today in light of the hard-won wisdom of the memories, stories, and scripts from the past.

This practice borrows from an exercise I experienced on a retreat nearly three years ago. The framework is connected to the practice of examen, a practice of Ignatian spirituality.[11] While there are many forms of the examen, including one that requires a thirty-day retreat,[12] this practice is built for ease of use at any time.

- First, pray and acknowledge the presence of God's Spirit. Take some time in silence to let any swirling thoughts settle (as much as they can).

- Second, name some things you're grateful for. Specifically, bring to mind the memory or memories you have had in mind throughout your reading. Holding a painful memory in gratitude may be difficult, so perhaps express gratitude for the way God has worked redemption out of that memory.

- Third, pay attention to any emotion that comes up as you bring that memory to mind. We will speak more about memories and emotions in chapter eight, so you may need to return to this practice at a later time. Express those emotions to God, and notice any lessons that these emotions bring to mind.

- Finally, allow yourself some time to pray this question: "God, how can you turn this memory and the experience of it into wisdom for my immediate future?" Or "How are you calling me to pass on the wisdom that I have gained from this memory or story?"

8

I'VE FELT LIKE
THIS BEFORE

The religious mind involves the whole of man, embraces his relations
with time within their true ground and setting in the Eternal Lover.

THOMAS KELLY

*M*usic has a power over us, to be sure. Songs in their own way
can serve as midwives for memories. Many of our memories have a soundtrack, and that soundtrack infuses our stories
and scripts.

Songs and poems can carry emotions and energies that words
alone can't. They are hymns of celebration and memorable ways
to engage in recollections that we'd often rather forget. We have
no problem remembering the lyrics to both.

In the discussion about how memories influence our spiritual
formation, the poetic beauty of the Psalms turns memories into
something more.

They are songs of remembrance of our humanity.

They are songs of frustration with our fellow humans.

They are gifts of peace in seasons when peace is in short supply.

They often partner memories with emotion.

The hippocampus is the part of our brain that serves as the routing station for our memories. And without a functioning hippocampus we cannot "form new memories, store new information, or stimulate the senses to evoke emotion."[1] Truly, our memories are not just details and places; they are also keyed to significant emotions.

Lisa Feldman Barrett observes,

> Emotions are not reactions to the world. You are not a passive receiver of sensory input but an active constructor of your emotions. From sensory input and past experience, your brain constructs meaning and prescribes action. If you didn't have concepts that represent your past experience, all your sensory inputs would just be noise.[2]

There is one song that brims with memory and emotion for me. It captures a year of life that would teach me—and as a carried memory continues to form me—of the paradoxical way of living with God in the world.

The song is "Sultans of Swing" by Dire Straits. It also brings to mind the power, presence, and poetry of the Psalms.

FAITH MEETS FEELING

While scrolling through Twitter recently, I saw a tweet promoting a sermon series called "Finding Fulfillment: Living by Faith, not Feelings." Of course without knowing the content, it is hard to say how this theme is fleshed out, but my initial thought on the topic was, *I imagine there won't be much content from the Psalms in that series.*

The Psalms are brilliant, beautifully musical poetry that dives into the complexity of life with God. They are not sanitized or edited, they do not come with warning labels, and they most definitely are not doctrinal statements. They are poems that evoke, challenge, and inspire our emotions.

The Psalms come from the memory of a people haunted by God's grace and promise, but they also connect with our memories of what it means to be human and to *feel* that reality. This is an incredible gift of God to us: our emotions find a historical connection to the story of God in the world. This is why the Psalms are critical for formation—they connect to the narrative of our lives on a level where we *feel* the story developing.

"Singing marks spiritual passages—both the formal ones of birth, marriage, and death, and the informal ones of commitment, doubt, and renewal." Musicians Don and Emily Saliers think of music as "soul practice" because music awakens "our souls to matters beyond the ordinary." Truly, "music is not simply an ornament of something already understood in words. Rather, ordered sound mediates the world to our senses and animates—literally ensouls—those who enter it deeply."[3]

We experience the Psalms deeply because we've felt what they convey, and we remember those feelings. In fact, the Hebrew word *zkr* or "remember" appears 169 times in the Bible, typically with either God or Israel as the subject.[4] The vast majority of those appearances are found in the Psalms.

It's fascinating that the emotive poetry of the Psalms matches our own memories of suffering, struggle, joy, and excitement. These poems beg us and the God of all creation to *remember*.

We remember disappointment. We remember feeling abandoned. We remember feeling rescued. Those feelings rather than hindering faith tend to catalyze, shape, and invigorate our faith.

Since our memories are not simply facts and details, I, as a spiritual director, can faithfully guide someone by saying, "Remember how you felt." Researchers Elizabeth Johnston and Leah Olson say that emotions come from neurological systems that "act to provide meaning and value to the information being processed."[5]

> *The emotive poetry of the Psalms matches our own memories of suffering, struggle, joy, and excitement. These poems beg us and the God of all creation to remember.*

Just as the stories born from our memories provide a structure for our life in the world with God, our emotions emerge from those memories as essential pieces that shape and direct us.

A SONG FOR WINTER

I remember the late spring of 1996. As the sun was sinking I twirled my key ring on my finger, half out of anxiety and half out of habit, as I walked the length of the parking lot to my car. In my final high school semester, I was working at an afterschool program at my church. I was the sports guy. I was also the de facto janitor. It was a job.

That spring I had difficulty keeping my mind on something other than what was happening at home.

The previous winter my dad had moved out of our house into another not far away. The moment has become a turning point in my life, a Moses-like memory where I was stripped of something I had long believed was eternal, unbreakable. It is helpful to remember that not everything shaved away from our souls in the wilderness is *false*.

What I remember most about that winter scene is the snow. A small U-Haul truck pulled into our driveway, split possessions were loaded into the back, and snow fell without regard for the events transpiring underneath. Strange how little the weather cares about our personal crises.

When I return to that memory today, a psalm comes to mind: "The LORD is my shepherd, I shall not want" (Ps 23:1). It's the first line of a song written by a man named David, a shepherd in his own right. The lyric reaches into a deep well of memories about crisis and conflict and darkness that all humans can sympathize with, only to come out with a firm belief in care and provision.

In the falling snow of January 1996, the stimuli of cold and moving and absence generated not only details and facts that are now stored in my long-term memory but also an emotion: helplessness.

We feel helplessness and wonder, *Who will help me? Who will provide in the absence of this person (or place or thing) that gave me meaning and light and life?* David meets the emotion of help-lessness with the poetic strength that Eugene Peterson presents as "God, my shepherd! I don't need a thing" (Ps 23:1 *The Message*).

The psalm pictures God moving into the low position of a shepherd, a station well below his divine privilege. And in that move he provides for people in a complete and all-encompassing way. At least, that's what it was intended to do.

Memories of need are stories of hardship, times when some-thing expected is diminished or falls through.

A job loss leads to bills piling up.

A partnership with a spouse disintegrates, leaving an emo-tional and financial void.

Or the person we expected to grow old with leaves a physical vacuum, and our feelings on the matter mold and remold our brain tissue.

Of course, that experience creates a memory. The memory of betrayal and abandonment in a marriage comes quickly, but with it comes the memory of immediate and intense need. The need for provision may bring with it the desire to solve the crisis "by any means necessary." We are ready to sacrifice whatever it takes to meet our obligations.

The temptation is to take the emotion ebbing from those shells and create a new story, a story of isolation. *If I don't look out for myself, who will? No one else can be trusted or depended on.* The script then writes itself.

When we remember the Shepherd, however, the emotion of receiving his provision helps shape our brains from isolation to interdependence with God. We memorize Psalm 23 to attach emotions to information, and we learn the wisdom of feeling our faith.

As David Seamands notes, "In fact, our feelings about God can drastically affect our ideas of God. This is because those feelings are part of the dynamics which determine the way we perceive the teachings given to us."[6]

In my emotional engagement with the psalms, Psalm 131 has been particularly helpful, especially verse 2:

> I have calmed and quieted my soul,
>> like a weaned child with its mother;
>> my soul is like the weaned child that is with me.

The child is not demanding its mother's milk but is free to be present without expectations.

It is the true and simple love of presence for presence's sake. I felt that emotion. The emotion of being cared for by *presence*, not by *providing tangible substance*. To have sensed God's presence in the past without expectation sustains us when our present expectations for life, death, family, work, and relationships go unsatisfied.

We can't be formed fully by the promise of God's provision if we can't connect with the feeling of being cared and provided for by God, which means we have to learn the language of emotions.

FUNERAL MEMORIES

For many of us, Psalm 23 draws us back to a funeral. The reason the psalm is a graveside comfort is not because it distracts us from the casket and mortality. Instead, it points to the reality of death and the God who both enters and supersedes it.

The power of the Psalms is not that they settle us with otherworldly anthems, but they move us toward our emotions about the temporary and the eternal, and in the middle we find *reality*. To be formed by the Spirit of Jesus is above all to deal with reality, which means our memories and the resulting emotions. Too often we are given a choice—emotions or faith and belief. Yet as Dan Allender and Tremper Longman observe,

> Emotion links our internal and external worlds. To be aware of what we feel can open us to questions we would rather ignore. . . .
>
> Ignoring our emotions is turning our back on reality; listening to our emotions ushers us into reality. And reality is where we meet God. . . . In neglecting our intense emotions, we are false to ourselves and lose a wonderful opportunity

to know God. We forget that change comes through brutal honesty and vulnerability before God.[7]

Many of us meet the reality of God in the vulnerability of the Psalms, and in my experience many people have an encounter with God at a funeral.

WHERE ARE YOU?

Just after the snowy incident with the U-Haul mentioned earlier, a high school acquaintance committed suicide on Super Bowl Sunday.

When I walked into the high school cafeteria on the following Monday morning, the air itself felt heavy and dark. Having spent the previous evening watching the game with friends, I had no idea of what had happened. When I heard the news, emotion naturally rose to the surface.

I felt vulnerable, fragile, and isolated. It is challenging to be suddenly confronted with emotions regarding a person I hadn't spoken with in a week. We were not close, but suddenly the fragility of our humanness brought us together. It was a reminder that we both could die. I cannot think of that chilly February Monday without that same emotion coming to the surface.

David moves from provision to stating a reality, "Even though I walk through the darkest valley" (Ps 23:4). The reality is that even though we are provided for, this does not exempt us from the darkest valleys. The same shepherd king, David, also wrote Psalm 22, a song of absence, isolation, and fragility: "My God, my God, why have you forsaken me?" (v. 1).

When we read this, we think of Jesus suffering execution on the cross. At the crucial moment when Jesus bent the wheel of history away from power and toward love, he chose a line from the shared hymnal of humanity that remembers God's absence.

When we are face to face with pain, with loss, and with our own emotional valleys, it is impossible to imagine God being *present* in those circumstances. The memories and stories of God, even from Psalm 23:1, would say that a God who provides cannot be present in absence.

Yet that is David's and others' experience, echoed best in the phrase, "How long, O LORD" (see Ps 13:1; 35:17).

When the psalmists cry out "How long, O LORD," they are pleading for deliverance and feeling impatient and frustrated, but beneath that there is something much deeper. They are impatient and frustrated because they have experienced his deliverance in the past. They have a shell, a memory, a story, a script that says, "God is a deliverer. Act accordingly." This is not a new request or a new reality.

When we feel God's absence, it creates *dissonance*—the memories, scripts, and stories are failing. We knew God as the Father who stayed close, we knew our thirsts quenched and anxieties quelled by the great Shepherd, but we now feel like a dry riverbed. Where has the source of life gone?

At the moment when Jesus turned death inside out by ingesting it while suffering on the cross, the emotion of that moment pushed him to cry, "'My God, my God, why have you forsaken me?" (Mt 27:46).

As I fumbled with my necktie, I noted that I was running late for the funeral service for my high school acquaintance. I wrestled with my own forsaken emotion, which Frederick Buechner gives voice to:

My God, where the Hell are you, meaning if thou art our Father who art in Heaven, be thou also our Father who art in Hell because Hell is where the action is, where I am and the cross is. It is where the pitiless storm is. It is where men labor and are heavy laden under the burden of their own lives without you. Where they cut themselves shaving and smoke three packs a day though they know the surgeon general's warning by heart.[8]

The words of forsakenness shape us to meet reality—the emotion that comes when we walk through the darkest valley, when we intellectually meet the thoughts of the teacher in Ecclesiastes:

"Meaningless! Meaningless!"
    says the Teacher.
"Utterly meaningless!
    Everything is meaningless." (Ecclesiastes 1:2 NIV)

The Hebrew word for "meaningless" is *hebel*.[9] Meaninglessness isn't just a thought or an idea, however. It is tinted with feeling, the helplessness and despair at the root of *hebel* best translated as "This is pointless."

The emotion of *hebel* in the Psalms, the song of dark valleys and forsaken places, isn't supposed to be justified or explained or systematized. Instead, we are invited to feel *hebel*, to know it well enough to point it out like a familiar face on a crowded street.

Sitting at the funeral mass for a seventeen-year-old has the scent of *hebel*, which has formed me to know that there will be times when provision comes in dark spaces.

In my memory, it is as if the incense still flows around me, with flowers dotting the rising concrete seams in the cathedral. To my right it looks like third-period biology; to my left, senior English. My classmates surround me, their hands all holding a shell that represents this moment, and it will never leave them. Meaningless. The snow falls; we leave the church and our eyes drop to the ground as the sun pierces through the cold. We hug each other and head home for the day because attending classes is simply too much to ask on a day like this.

As we learn to be formed by engaging our memories, stories, and scripts, we will benefit from the way Psalms teach us to turn our collar against the cold and call the valley what it is—*hebel*. Granted, Psalm 23:4 gives us a gentle gift in the aftermath of the dark valley:

> Even though I walk through the darkest valley,
> I fear no evil,
>   for you are with me.

Formation through our memories reminds us there are times when we will speak of the valley through shouting and gritted teeth, but we may remember speaking of fearlessness and God's presence with only a whisper.

Which makes complete sense. Every memory belongs.

THE FEELING OF COLLISION

Back to the church parking lot. I walk to the car twirling my key ring after an early spring afternoon at work. The scent of floor cleaner is still fresh in my nostrils, as are the details of the tumultuous winter behind me.

Once I was clear of the church building, I had the quiet of my own presence and began a personal monologue. Walking to the car I began to think about my future life: college was looming on the horizon, including training for my future ministry, and my girlfriend would be attending the same college. Of course, before that there would be a graduation ceremony, parties, and all the rites of passage for which I, at the moment, felt ill prepared.

How do I remember these details so clearly and with such emotion rising even as I write? I struggle to remember day-to-day events; how do these items come with such clarity?

Lisa Feldman Barrett asks the same question: "Why do some memories, such as this memory

As we learn to be formed by engaging our memories, stories, and scripts, we will benefit from the way Psalms teach us to turn our collar against the cold and call the valley what it is—hebel, "meaningless."

about an intensely emotional experience, seem to persist in vivid detail for years, while others seem much less detailed and fade over time? William James in an oft-quoted statement claimed that 'an experience may be so exciting as to almost leave a scar on the cerebral tissue.'"[10]

Our brain is often a strange and unpredictable gift to our souls.

Studies on the effects of traumatic or challenging events on the brain show "the mind works according to schemes or maps, and incidents that fall outside the established pattern are most likely to capture our attention."[11] In turn, the research of Dr. James McGaugh and his colleagues shows that the more adrenaline you secrete, the more precise your memory.

Intense experiences, both the dark and forsaken moments and those of timely provision, create intense emotions, and the heightened attention fastens these events deep in our brains.

They are the shells we collect, the memories and stories that have a hand in making us who we are today.

I climbed into the car. First the key, then the clutch, and then the gas.

I began to speak the circumstances of my life out loud, alone, in my car as I rolled through the church parking lot and up the gradual incline to a stop sign. Traffic blurred by, and I talked of life and death and family to the metronome of my turn signal.

The sun set to my left, just at the crest of the hill. It gave the impression that the oncoming traffic was blasted from the core of the sun itself. I would need to turn left across two lanes of traffic, which was problematic. The brightness saturated my vision, or at least that's what I believe happened. It is how I remember it.

I engaged the waltz of gas, brake, and clutch, and pulled into traffic only to hear the squeal of tires and the sound of metal and plastic crunching just behind my left ear.

I never saw the car approaching from my left. Perhaps I lost it in the sun. Perhaps I was simply distracted. I don't remember, ironic as that might be.

I remember being distracted by the feeling of the moment. I remember the feeling of drowning; of course, I wasn't drowning, but I felt as if I was lost in my own life, and a strange joy came suddenly as I looked at everything around me.

Thoughts began to roll, but more than that, emotions began to pour out: the feelings of guilt ("I'm going to lose my license"), failure ("I can't believe I did that"), anger ("Are you kidding me? Now *this*?"), and gratitude ("I'm still here. I see the people from the other car—*they're still here.*")

The reality of physics is that had the car hit six inches to the left, or had I pulled out a millisecond earlier, the collision would have engaged the driver's side door and my body. I would have been irrevocably changed.

At that very moment I noticed the Dire Straits song "Sultans of Swing" blaring through the speakers in my car. The song was instantly attached to my memory of that moment. It brings me back to that moment sitting frozen in my car, perpendicular to the center line on the road. The song takes me back to a moment when I simultaneously asked, *What else could possibly go wrong this year?* and thought, *I am happy to be alive.*

At that moment something became clear to me that I can only give words to now. It is a realization that naturally arose from my exploration of the year that was 1996. As previously stated, our memories give rise to our stories and scripts and the emotions attached, but what I realized is this: to write a psalm and convey the emotions related to our memories of life with God, we must first *live* the psalm.

As the spring of 1996 closed, I feel I could have written with confidence, "God, my shepherd! I don't need a thing. Even though I walk through the darkest valley, I will fear no evil for you are with me."

Perhaps the greatest gift we have is to *feel* our emotions faithfully—to engage our memories and feel whatever rises to the surface.

Perhaps the next step in our formation in the way of Jesus is to let the skin we live in feel, and to remember the feeling and allow the music of our disciplines and the Psalms guide us into a new story and script in the future.

PRACTICE

As we saw in this chapter, the Psalms are memories of human emotion. We can't truly write or love a psalm until we remember what it feels like to *live* that psalm.

This practice is to help us write a psalm based on our own key memories. The purpose is to fully engage the emotions associated with those memories. The psalm we write does not have to be shown to anyone else, and it is important that we pay attention to any feelings of vulnerability or even embarrassment that may come with putting these emotions in print.

The point in writing is not to present a sanitary version of the story. As the Psalms themselves testify, the expression of emotions out of our memories is often painful and incisive, even toward God himself.

- Set aside some time for this practice. Rushing this kind of work can be counterproductive. Anywhere from fifteen to thirty minutes is a good starting point. Acknowledge God's presence as you begin this exercise. Remind yourself that God is not insulted by your emotional responses or experiences.

- Before you begin writing your own psalm, it helps to prepare by reading a few psalms. Try Psalms 13, 22, 23, 35, and 131. It also may be helpful for you to have the spiritual autobiography you wrote earlier nearby for reflection and reminders.

- Recall a memory you have been processing throughout this book and try to express the emotions that come to mind as you engage it. You may use the emotion you named in chapter one or another that has taken a place of prominence in your mind. Write down each emotion that arises, any questions that are connected to that event or emotion, and any image that comes to mind as you revisit that memory.

- Attempt to format your emotions regarding the memory in the form of a poem. It does not have to rhyme nor does it have to be perfect. But the important pieces of unfiltered emotion and symbolism could help you see these emotions differently.
- When you feel you've clearly captured the emotions of that memory, read what you've written, preferably out loud. Listen to the words as you pronounce them, hearing whatever may be left below the surface.
- In silent prayer, ask God what moments of formation, redemption, or redirection are necessary for the way you feel about that memory. Remember again that God is just as present now as he was in the original event, and nothing that can happen at this moment will change this reality.

9

A FAMILIAR TABLE

*The ideal of the spiritual life in the Christian understanding is one
where all of the essential parts of the human self are effectively
organized around God, as they are restored and sustained by him.*

Dallas Willard

My wife and I had the same dining room table in our house for a long time. The table was a result of a somewhat countercultural approach to our wedding. Instead of investing all the money we were given in the ceremony and reception, we skipped on a few amenities and instead invested part of the money in furniture.

It was a wise investment. That furniture lasted for nearly fourteen years.

Our dining table was simple: the legs and surface support structures were painted white and artificially distressed. The top was a light oak grain, with a slit in the center to pull the table apart and insert a leaf that turned seating for four into seating for six (or perhaps a tight eight).

While we had that table, we shared space with a variety of folks over the years. We sat over steaming bowls of pasta, passed warm baskets of bread, and finished with my wife's incredible homemade apple pies and other delicacies. While we feasted, we also listened.

We ate with a friend heading on a new journey, with everything he owned sitting in the back of his truck. He was walking the way of St. Francis, Rich Mullins, and other pilgrims to find "the wideness in God's mercy / I cannot find in my own."[1]

We ate with a couple who twisted shiny new wedding bands on their fingers, talking about finances and family, only to later learn that their journey of "dancing in the minefields" of marriage did not last.[2]

We hosted family from near and far, celebrating new opportunities with clinking glasses and processing letting go of the past and moving on to new adventures.

Those meals around our simple table disarmed me. Those moments of eating together, of inviting someone into our home, feel like they happened yesterday.

Do you have these shells? Do you know this table?

Tables are places where memories are created. I have learned that from my own practice, but also from the story of Jesus.

THE JESUS AT THE TABLE

Jesus revealed the hospitality of God to the world. Christine Pohl in *Making Room* writes, "By definition, hospitality involves some space into which people are welcomed, a place where unless the invitation is given, the stranger would not feel free to enter."[3]

Jesus says, "Very truly, I tell you, the Son can do nothing on his own, but only what he sees the Father doing; for whatever the Father does, the Son does likewise" (Jn 5:19). Discovering this, we collect a shell that reveals the nature of God through the hospitality of Jesus. God, in fact, has a wide and open table. In other words, Jesus is the host and hospitality requires the host to be *present*. We then are invited into the presence of our host.

We do not find it difficult to remember the places where we have not been welcomed, where our memories, stories, and scripts have not been given a place. Some of our stories and scripts are based on a table that requires merit, stature, or resources. Some of us believe that we are only one *grace* or one *goodness* away from a place of our own at God's great and rich table. Those stories are critiqued, exposed, and debunked by the life of Jesus.

In fact, as we remember Jesus in the Gospels, we encounter his hospitality of presence. We remember Jesus sharing meals, the lifeblood of communities in that culture, with people who could not advance an agenda or contribute to a campaign.

Jesus formed memories, stories, and scripts by inviting people to a table.

Jesus' hospitality of presence creates an infinite, even eternal, loop. Whenever we sit down to bread and wine together, or when we see others across the row or around the circle in our faith communities who are about to reenter an ancient memory, we know we are not alone either in the present or in the sweeping arc of history.

The crimson liquid in the cup reminds us of the execution of an innocent man at the hands of a panicked empire that knew Jesus was too free to be allowed to live. He invites us to be with him, to be like him and walk as sweaty miracles in this world (Jn 14:12). It is a beautiful reality that begins with the hospitality of presence.

How do we integrate our own shells into Jesus' hospitality of presence? How does the hospitality of presence shape our formation through Jesus?

The work of Christian spiritual formation (formation around Jesus within the skin we're in) finds its root, energy, and purpose in the revolutionary carpenter Son of God, who beat death and opened the grave to new life. The work of spiritual formation is always formation toward something, and our memories have formed us for an encounter with this Jesus.

What does this look like in light of our shells?

At a critical moment in my own journey, I rediscovered Jesus through the words and influence of a Dutch Catholic priest, Henri Nouwen. For a long time Jesus to me had been a disembodied figure, a piece of divinity who dallied in humanity long enough to set things right, die, rise, and depart. I was encouraged to see my own guilt in the crucifixion but not to discover my blessedness as a witness to his life and teaching.

Nouwen's book *Life of the Beloved* brought the story and reality of Jesus into my vision in a new way.[4]

Nouwen uses the Eucharist metaphor—Jesus' movement of *taking* the bread, *blessing* it, *breaking* it, and *giving* it—to reinvigorate our memories of the life Jesus lived and consequently the story of our formation through Jesus in this world.

The taking, blessing, breaking, and giving serves as a kind of decoder ring for our memories. Placed over the long arc of our lives, we see our various shells in light of Jesus' story. The hope is that our scripts would be transformed through the radical and poetic recall of these images.

We begin by being *taken*.

YOUR OWN PLACEMAT

When my wife and I got married, I entered into a new family. As a person with deep ties to his own biological family, I felt off-balance for a few years. The expectations and guidelines for a family are often difficult to discover and take time and repetition to truly understand.

It is interesting after being a part of that new family for nearly twenty years to think now about the awkwardness I felt early on.

A moment occurred during our first Christmas, however, that turned the script in a different direction. During Christmas, my in-laws put out different placemats. They were decades-old collages of several different Christmas cards taped together and laminated to form a unique and personalized placemat.

At our first Christmas, I came to the table and saw that I had my own placemat. It was more significant for me than my family may have known. It was the moment when my transition became official. I was taken from the billions of human beings in the world and given a specific place at the table.

Jesus' power is in taking people from randomness and obscurity and moving them into the light for the sake of telling a new story about God's work in the world.

Jesus' power is in *taking* people from randomness and obscurity and moving them into the light for the sake of telling a new story about God's work in the world. He is changing scripts and memories every time he resists the common charge to separate, distinguish, and alienate.

He takes a leper and makes him clean, which first requires Jesus sharing the leper's presence (Mt 8:2). He takes a Samaritan—symbolically through a story of compassion—and brings him into the pantheon of folk heroes (Lk 10:30-37). He takes a criminal, executed by the state for insurrection, much as Jesus was, and invites him into paradise despite the criminal's questionable résumé (Lk 23:43).

We cannot experience and memorize the stories of Jesus without seeing his radical *inclusion*—taking those who were left on the edges of society, left to their own solitude, and bringing them into his kingdom.

We often forget what it feels like to be drawn in from what the Bible calls "far country" (Lk 15:13 ESV).

Around your and my dining tables, those who eat with us were *invited*. Jesus' action of *taking* is one of selecting and inviting, and the broadness of that invitation gives hope to our memories. Regardless of our shells of absence and exclusion, Jesus' life offers presence and inclusion—we are invited.

Henri Nouwen describes Jesus' invitation this way: "To be chosen as the Beloved of God is something radically different [from our version of being chosen]. Instead of excluding others, it includes others. Instead of rejecting others as less valuable, it accepts others in their own uniqueness. It is not a competitive, but a compassionate choice."[5]

Remember that spiritual formation is not a hostile takeover by an all-powerful deity. It is the wooing of One who shared existence in flesh *with us*. Formation is remembering that there is no journey that God has not mapped in Jesus (Heb 4:15-16), and that to be *taken* is to be caught up in Jesus' response to our common challenges and quests.

To learn Jesus' life in skin as an apprentice—as a carpenter learns the way of planed boards and finishing nails—is to learn the comely and revolutionary life of discipleship. The call to live deeply in the kingdom of God as an apprentice of Jesus makes no sense if Jesus the master teacher instructs us in a way that is irrelevant to our everyday lives.

Our lives in the world as God intends requires people who are intoxicated by their *takenness* in Jesus and who remember that *takenness* in the light of the way Jesus embraced it in the past.

THE BLESSING OF PRESENCE

Jesus' life on earth is an artistic display of God in skin, and the canvas is our memory. Into this life and these teachings, we are invited, like the first disciples, to "abide" (Jn 15:1-5).

Abiding, writes Lesslie Newbigin, "is the continually renewed decision that what has been done once for all by the action of Jesus shall be the basis, the starting point, the context for all my thinking and deciding and doing."[6]

We are blessed with the invitation to abide in the *taking* movement of Jesus so we might be with him. This welcome lodges in our long-term memory because in a world of separation, the adrenaline attached to the memory is strong enough to leap across our synapses with the greatest of ease.

We need this memory most when we're standing in line at the grocery store, being berated by our supervisor, or staring at the lines in our face enhanced by the dark season we currently inhabit.

Remembering our takenness by Jesus reminds us that we have a *place*, and that place crafts our stories and our scripts. Any healthy spiritual practice of remembering will bring us back to the truth that we are taken for something greater than what we have known.

My grandfather used to take me out to his shed where he kept a variety of wonders, mostly old radios and electrical parts, and we'd pretend we were the commanders of a spacecraft rocketing to parts unknown.

Mostly he watched and laughed while I shouted and turned knobs in desperate attempts to avoid alien conquest. This is also where I learned how to swear. It's all part of intergalactic warfare, apparently.

He taught me several Southern phrases I have never forgotten: "frog strangler," for example, is a phrase that describes a heavy rainstorm. I can't repeat many of the others because I've trusted them into the care of grandfather-grandson confidentiality.

I remember those phrases because I remember my grandfather as a person. His mischievous energy would later turn to a deep quiet, and then that quiet would lead him to nap relatively unnoticed as the years of his life ended. His phrases likely wouldn't make sense to you because you had to know the world they came from.

I know him through presence—his presence with me and mine with him.

I miss him through absence—the ache of my self-removal and his natural departure.

To the left of my desk is a shelf where I see my grandfather's King James Version Bible. I don't remember my grandfather being a particularly religious man spouting spiritual wisdom or guidance, but that Bible is *presence* for me.

There is something about a physical presence that reminds us of someone we have lost track of or are missing. It is a reminder of what is beyond us now. It is the incarnation—the *enfleshing*—of a reality.

True hospitality is impossible if the host isn't at the table.

Jesus' *taking* people like you and me isn't an invitation to be okay in some loose sense. We are taken for a purpose. We are invited to be blessed ones in the presence of the Host.

SIGN HERE PLEASE

We have a new dining table now. The wedding-gift table wore down, and the chairs began to break, which is quite opposite to the idea of hospitality.

"We have a chair for you, but please keep your movements to a minimum."

The new table is a darker stain, sturdy, built over what seemed like a year by Amish craftsmen. It is the definition of durable.

My wife and I agreed to a new tradition when the table came to our home. A friend introduced us to the idea of having dinner guests sign the bottom of the table with a Sharpie. So we began inviting people to dinner and—when we remembered, as ironic as that is—we would hand them a black, green, or red Sharpie and ask them to sign the table.

Good friends and new friends, their stomachs full, lay on their backs under the table while still attempting to look presentable. We now have signatures from our new friend Mandy Harvey, a singer who lost her hearing at eighteen yet went on to finish in second place on *America's Got Talent*. We have the drawings and well-wishes of friends from Chicago and Arizona. We even have the autograph from a long-time friend who, apparently giddy with excitement, misspelled her own name.

To be invited to the table is one thing. To be given permission to lovingly vandalize the furniture of others is quite another. In

Nouwen's metaphor, this practice could be called a *blessing*. It is not only welcome but giving a gift that says, "We want to remember that you were here, and now you have a place here permanently."

Blessedness is a state of being spoken well of. It is difficult to find a greater sign of blessing than to welcome a name in permanent marker on the bottom of your table.

Our story of formation begins with being taken, redeeming the shells of separation and absence, and being invited into a story of having a seat at the table. However, another shell falls into our hands from the words of Jesus, "You are no longer servants [chosen] you are now friends [wanted and welcome]" (Jn 15:15, my paraphrase).

Blessing reminds us that the invitation to the table catalyzes the blessing of being there, of being worthy and beautiful and good because we are followers of Jesus. The poetry of Genesis that says, "Let us make humankind in our image," and that all of creation is "very good" (Gen 1:26, 31) comes to a head when Jesus invites all of us to the table not as guests but as friends. We feel the weight of the words of Emilie Griffin: "We who are made in his image are also incredibly old; if not eternal, we have nevertheless been present in his mind for a very long time, if not surely from the beginning. In any event, the Lord has always longed for us; he has lived for us and looked forward eagerly to our response."[7]

We stop the flow of trying to deserve God, whatever that may mean. Our memory of Jesus helps rewrite our personal memories, stories, and scripts in light of not only being invited to abide but blessed and wanted.

Jesus moves from *taking* the bread, helping the disciples see their bodies as something critical in the unfolding narrative of God, to *naming* it. The movement to the true self is often catalyzed by remembering our name, understanding who we are and grasping a larger identity. "He took a loaf of bread, and after *blessing* it . . ." (Mk 14:22).

The bread is taken, but it is only bread at that point. Choosing does not recreate the bread, but the blessing reminds everyone of the bread's goodness. The most difficult thing to do with our memories, our stories, is to speak goodness over them.

To see our memories as good is not to deny their darkness but to see where and how Jesus brings the light. Bread is imperfect, perhaps overly kneaded and hard in places, but when we speak good over it—when we bless it—we give it a quality of life that says, "Regardless of imperfection, this imperfect thing is good here and now." It is bringing light out of something common, even something painful.

ANYTHING BUT BLESSED

The blessing is also critical because taking without blessing is simply tolerance. We remember that we are not chosen and tolerated because that seems like the right thing to do, but we are instead blessed and wanted and spoken well of.

So many of us live with stories in which we have been anything *but* blessed by those around us. We have been taken—we've been called husband, wife, son, daughter, friend—but we have not felt the soft beauty of blessing at those tables.

What is fascinating about this concept of blessing is how quickly we adopt names based on our experiences, memories, stories, and scripts. Failure names us. Abuse names us. A sexual reputation names us. We name ourselves, and we take on the names others give us.

The best way to examine this is to meditate on the ideas that protest our attempting something new. A voice often comes up that says, "You can't do that. You're a failure. You're too anxious, too young, too everything opposite of what you need to be for this. You are not enough."

Henri Nouwen indicates that this is precisely why our memories need to be blessed. He observes, "I am increasingly aware of how much we fearful, anxious, insecure human beings are in need of a blessing." A blessing is so powerful because "a blessing goes beyond the distinction between admiration or condemnation, between virtues or vices, between good deeds or evil deeds. A blessing touches the original goodness of the other and calls forth his or her Belovedness."[8]

Only blessing allows us to continue the journey through our memories knowing that regardless of how our past may describe us, it is our chosenness and our blessedness that defines us.

For me as a person who has battled with addiction in the past, to be spoken well of—to be blessed—is to remember that the darkest parts of my journey to this point are not damnation and cursing but *inventory*.

Memory researchers reveal that memory and creativity are linked historically.

The Latin root *inventio* is the basis for two words in our modern English vocabulary: *inventory* and *invention*. And to a mind trained in the art of memory, those two ideas were closely linked. Invention was a product of inventorying. . . . In order to invent, one first needed a proper inventory, a bank of existing ideas to draw on.[9]

In spaces and relationships that do not help us remember our blessedness, we need to creatively reimagine our lives as those welcomed and blessed at the table.

The shells created in my memory regarding addiction are now part of my story of redemption and forgiveness, which I can revisit without helplessness. They create a collection of terms such as *rock bottom* or *guilt* or *recovery* with which I can now weave together a more beautiful tapestry. Engaging my shells with the welcome of Jesus, I see these pieces of inventory not as determining my future but as ripe for redemption in my present-day journey with Jesus.

When we remember, we are both taken and blessed. We then can take dark memories and bring blessing out of their seemingly opaque narratives.

In spaces and relationships that do not help us remember our blessedness, we need to creatively reimagine our lives as those welcomed and blessed at the table. If not, the ideas of being taken and blessed fade and are replaced by a far more destructive image.

TEAR OFF A PIECE

I look back on many of my childhood memories and see them through a different cognitive frame. I no longer look at family fights or other social situations as a child. I remember times when my parents would snicker about something quietly, and when I asked, "What's so funny?" they would say, "Oh, nothing," and move on with sheepish grins on their faces. Looking back on such situations, I now can see the threads that met in their grins and realize, "Oh, that's what was going on there."

With perspective, we remember differently. We also clearly see some basic tints of our human, and therefore spiritual, lives. We understand generosity because we see it in the bigger picture. We understand faith because it grows into a tidal wave throughout our lives with both God and others.

We also remember brokenness because we see broken things; we feel them just as deeply now as we did in days gone by. Brokenness is a magnetic memory because it draws our attention and holds our gaze. It does not matter which pole the brokenness is drawn to: from us to others, from others to us, or even from our hearts to God.

Our memories give us an opportunity to see how, like the bread, we are chosen for something beautiful and spoken well of by God, but our experience also yields another memory: "after blessing it he broke it" (Mk 14:22).

To engage our memories as I am suggesting means that we need to wrestle with memories that reveal the darkest parts of humanity, ourselves, and in the way we perceive God.

Jesus' own life comes to the front here, reminding us that if he can say of the bread that "this is my body" (Mk 14:22), then our lives are both taken and blessed but also broken.

While Jesus lays down his own life, we do not have to hunt down brokenness. It comes unbidden. In his hospitality of presence, Jesus enters into a constant stream of human experience—brokenness of heart, mind, soul, and strength.

As we remember the life of Jesus on earth, we see a story and script that is adequate to deal with suffering. He who held resurrection like an ace under the table (Jn 11:17-44) also wept over the need to use that card to retrieve the life of Lazarus.

What Jesus experienced places suffering in a bigger context, namely that to take on our life, Jesus brought God's life into the realm of biology.

In breaking himself just as he breaks the bread, Jesus visually articulates hospitality for those who carry broken memories, stories, and scripts. Redemption of our memories takes place when, in the presence of Jesus, they are no longer seen as boundaries but as plot points in a greater drama— the drama of being taken and blessed, loved and longed for by God from the foundation of the world (Mt 25:34).

> *Jesus, the taken, blessed, and broken one, creates a memory for all of us, a miraculous memory that radically renovates the stories and scripts of the entire world.*

Jesus, the *taken, blessed,* and *broken* one, creates a memory for all of us, a miraculous memory that radically renovates the stories and scripts of the entire world.

The heart of the reality that every memory belongs comes screaming into view. To be taken and blessed without breaking is to live in some sort of ethereal realm, a place that truly doesn't exist. Yet Jesus forms us through remembering his own life in which we see that crosses often lead to joy (Heb 12:2), creating a connection between taking, blessing, and breaking.

The spiritual practice of remembering invites us to embrace our memories of brokenness. Nouwen says,

> Our brokenness is truly ours. Nobody else's. Our brokenness is as unique as our chosenness and our blessedness.

... Fearsome as it may sound, as the Beloved ones, we are called to claim our unique brokenness, just as we have to claim our unique chosenness and our unique blessedness.[10]

Our memories of walking upright in this world—in relationships, work, and spiritual growth—are filled with moments of transcendence as well as moments of tragedy. These moments are unique in detail, but they are also universal in theme. We don't have to travel far into our long-term memory to discover these events. In fact, they likely come to our minds on a regular basis without being invited.

When Jesus breaks the bread, he invites us to acknowledge that both the beautiful and the brutal memories belong. We see this in that at Jesus' table is a cast of flawed heroes (Mk 14). Peter could smell the bread, he could see the wine in the cup, and yet he would soon pretend he hadn't heard of Jesus (vv. 66-71).

Judas ate bread from the hand of Jesus, a hand that would be cruelly pierced by the words that would flow from Judas's lips.

Thomas reclined nearby, watching with a skeptical eye. Soon he would express doubt and seek evidence of the resurrection. "I need to touch and see," he would say (see Jn 20:24-28). Despite the miracles of multiplication and revival, Thomas thought resurrection was a bit beyond Jesus' pay grade.

Honestly, don't we all?

When Jesus breaks the bread and lets the light shine on the faces of those who were the first to follow and the first to abandon, we are invited into a greater drama where our acts of brokenness or our experiences of being broken by others are brought into sacred space.

FARM TO TABLE

The first church I pastored had a large table at the front of the sanctuary. I can see the faded bluish carpet and the green upholstery of the pews. I can see the worn spot in the back rail of a pew about three feet in on the right-hand side made by a farmer named David who had rubbed the spot bare over the years.

I see the paneled walls that formed the back of the room, and the white plaster arcing up toward the flat, white ceiling. There was a large painted scene behind our baptistery, supposedly of the Jordan River, and two massive green curtains that cupped the opening of the baptistery giving it a theatrical quality. I remember the controversy when I closed the curtains, just to change things up a bit.

The Communion table, however, is what I best remember. Every week we gathered and looked at the that table, where on the front just below the tabletop were inscribed the words, "Do this in remembrance of me" (Lk 22:19). The people, many who were hardened and hopeful farmers, came every week and ate the bread and drank the juice in *remembrance*. I, their pastor, the Southern boy with the ink still drying on his seminary degree, ate and drank with them in *remembrance*.

The idea that God would shape the imagination of humanity by revealing himself—vulnerable, graceful, and hospitable— through death at the hands of corrupt powers and authorities, is revolutionary. Jesus didn't die to satisfy some sick urge that his Father had for blood; instead, he died because our situation required a memory of God that would alter the previous myths we had believed.

You see, the core story of our formation in Jesus begins with *taken* and *blessed*; it doesn't begin with *broken*.

Taking the meal as remembrance of Jesus is incomplete if we forget that body and blood were taken and blessed before they were *ever* broken. Reconciliation of our memories comes when we embrace crucifixion, sure, but is also comes in the movement toward resurrection. Our pain can be reconciled to hope. All of us who share a body, whether physical or the mysterious body of Christ called church, can be reconciled to each other. Our memories of destruction can be meditations of peace in the present.

The moment when Jesus says, "Do this in remembrance of me," a great concussion was felt through history. In fact, the memories of liberation and failure in Exodus and Deuteronomy, as well as the presence and absence scripts we find in the Psalms, find a seat at this proverbial table.

Our woes and wins as parents, our gifts and gaffes as married people, our struggles and strides as young adults are all seated within the scent range of bread and wine.

Richard Rohr observes, "Once your life has become a constant communion, you know that all the techniques, formulas, sacraments and practices were just a dress rehearsal for the real thing—life itself—which can actually become a constant intentional prayer. Your conscious and loving existence gives glory to God."[11]

Through our beloved place at the table, bearing the memories and stories and scripts, we become a gift to the world. We're reminded that our brains have been designed by a beautiful Architect to hold tightly to *all things* (every memory belongs) and that in the meantime we are called to bless the world with a new story and a new script. Just as Jesus *gave* the bread to the disciples, he has given life to us. In turn, we are the conduit of giving new life to the world. It is a gift worth remembering.

What does this gift of the table mean for you? How have you brought your beloved self, broken in places, to this table so you may be formed for the story the Spirit of Jesus is catalyzing through the shells you carry?

May we begin to see our lives as built on experiences, memories, and stories cultivated in the presence of God. May we invite him to reveal through the scripts we live everyday into the healing, grace, and formation into Christlikeness that we desperately need.

PRACTICE

Hospitality, or any practice that flows out of the memory of the life of Jesus, is not accidental. We plan, we arrange, we set up our lives in the pursuit of it. Today, many of my friends cannot engage others because of the hectic whirlwind of their schedules. They have given their time to other things, and creating space for others to enter their lives at their tables or in backyards is nearly impossible.

In this practice, we engage our memories of being taken and blessed through welcoming others *in spite* of the way we are broken. I owe my wife a debt of gratitude for this practice; she is both thoughtful and compassionate when it comes to the use of our table.

- First, keep in mind that hospitality and sharing a meal doesn't need to be complicated. Banish the shells you've collected of home and garden magazines. Ordering takeout or using paper plates and cups is perfectly acceptable.

- The real power of hospitality—as we see in Jesus—is in the way we attend to others. As you decide who to invite, consider their needs, preferences, and personalities. Being invited to a table means being thought of in advance, and our guests feel blessed by their personal needs and preferences being considered.

- Be creative! Feel free to partner with someone else who has a gift or resource you do not. For example, if your table isn't big enough for the people you want to invite, consider partnering with someone who can accommodate that group.

- In preparing for the meal, bring to mind a memory of hospitality that was transformational to your story. The "placemat" story in this chapter is a good example. Consider sharing this story during the meal with your guests if you are comfortable doing so.

- Make the memory a moment of prayer for the people you are inviting. Pray that they might encounter Jesus' hospitality through presence at your table.
- Consider inviting your guests to sign the bottom of your table before they leave. Unless, of course, you're at someone else's house, in which case that's a bad idea.

10

REMEMBER, BE HERE NOW

I saw that, for me, this country would always be populated with presences and
absences, presences of absences, the living and the dead. The world as it is would
always be a reminder of the world that was, and of the world that is to come.

WENDELL BERRY

Guess where we are?"
I looked at my phone with curiosity. The text came from
a friend, with a picture attached. The curiosity level was com-
pounded by the fact that she was supposed to be part of a group
of friends at lunch with my wife celebrating Holley's birthday.

Clearly, the picture on my phone was of a tattoo parlor. The
group apparently hatched the idea at lunch and happily discovered nothing standing in the way of immediate execution. I
chuckled to myself.

My wife now has three tattoos, two that could be seen as reminders—memories written in ink on her skin. The first is the
phrase "be here now," written in my mother-in-law's lovely
cursive script. Holley has had this phrase as a spiritual guideline
for years, reminding her that the present moment is important no
matter how much we want to plan for and move toward the future.

The birthday tattoo is of three blackbirds on a branch. The birds reverberate Jesus' words: "Look at the birds of the air; they neither sow nor reap nor gather into barns, and yet your heavenly Father feeds them. Are you not of more value than they?" (Mt 6:26).

My wife's arms serve as a daily reminder of the tension of life with God here and now—we are called to follow Jesus in the *contingency* of the present moment, and in the process we build *resiliency* by hoping in God's future care yet to come.

These emblems represent a story that we desperately hope guides our script of formation in our marriage and family. It is also a memory and story that is built into one of the more unique books in the Bible, Revelation.

A VERY PRESENT FEAR

The sun cut lines through the windows of the classroom, dividing the green-and-beige tile floors that bore the treads of decades of students past.

I was teaching a class for freshman college students on how to read the Bible, and we had come to the book of Revelation. I asked for their perspectives on the book, "What do you think of when you think of Revelation?"

One student said, "I can't read it; it just scares me." I've heard many comments in the same vein—Revelation brings fear, uncertainty, anxiety, and unease to many contemporary readers. The nightmarish images and the detailed numerology present a challenge for modern Western readers. It is challenging especially to readers like me who grew up in a context where Revelation was read as a road map to the end of the world.

We read of and remember the wild images—beasts, harlots, and blood. Chaos. Destruction of life rooted in the here and now. We fear situations and circumstances that remind us of the devastators and power mongers of John's breathtaking imagery.

Revelation delivers the greatest challenge to human life, a challenge inseparable from spiritual life—death. We cannot read Revelation without gnawing through the intricacies of death itself.

In death we anticipate the end. In turn, Christian spiritual formation needs to help us understand the place of death in our lives.

Theologian Larry Rasmussen goes further, presenting a question that is at the heart of both our common reading of Revelation and our own sinew-straining wrestling match with death: "How do we order life together in a world with a nasty tendency to fall apart?"[1]

How can we "be here now" when the here and now is so fragile?

The visions of Revelation form a new framework for life and death and *everything* in between. In turn, these visions help a people facing death to understand life and everything else through a different lens. Rather than starting with keeping "avenger Jesus" (see Rev 19:11-16) happy, John crafts something very different.

Eugene Peterson sees John's purpose as demonstrating

a gospel order in the chaos of evil, and [arranging] the elements of experience and reason so that they are perceived proportionally and coherently: sin, defeat, discouragement, prayer, suffering, persecution, praise, and politics are placed in relation to the realities of God and Christ, holiness and healing, heaven and hell, victory and judgment, beginning and ending.[2]

The first audience for Revelation needed to be reminded of the coherence of all of the memories, stories, and scripts in Peterson's list above. It was a matter of life and death.

The churches of the Mediterranean world were finding their faith in King Jesus (the implied meaning of "Jesus Christ") at odds with Roman emperor Domitian, who demanded to be called *dominus et deus* or "Our Lord and Our God."[3]

In light of their struggle, the compassionate Christ inspired John with visions that would make sense to the Mediterranean churches in the midst of systemic and spiritual struggle. Keeping that in mind, we see John as a pastor was "writing with a passionate concern that ordinary men and women should understand what he had been charged to tell them, and, rightly or wrongly, he must have believed that they would be able to understand, . . . for a revelation would not be worth communicating if it did not transcend their previous knowledge."[4]

When we see all of the chaos of Revelation, we must remember all memories are both formed by and also form a context. The reign of Emperor Domitian, who believed all other gods were beneath him; the persecution that comes from living under such egotism; and the incisive pain of watching allegiance to the Prince of Peace lead to death; all of these realities form the backdrop for the visions themselves. Any future hope found in John's visions had to first and foremost address these gritty realities.

In light of what was coming, the early Christians in the Mediterranean needed reminders of how to be faithful in the present—to "be here now."

Michael Gorman says, "Revelation is not about the antichrist, but about the living Christ. It is not about a rapture out of this world but about faithful discipleship in this world."[5]

A LIVING LENS

John's introduction leads to seven letters to seven particular churches in the Mediterranean. They are in the darkness of Domitian but thirsty for a word that would bring them light and life.

The word to the first church—the "called-out ones" (*ekklēsia*) living against the steel of an empire—goes to those following Christ in the city of Ephesus (Rev 2:1-7). Ephesus has a familiar place in the Bible: Paul sent the church there a letter of great grace, a riot there put Paul's life in great danger, and a young pastor named Timothy served there under the encouragement of Paul to not be hindered by his youth.

Ephesus, in other words, was a place with presence and reputation.

The message to the church in Ephesus begins with that reputation, then moves to a sobering critique: "You have abandoned the love you had at first. Remember then from what you have fallen; repent, and do the works you did at first" (vv. 4-5).

Their return, the changing of their minds, which is at the heart of repentance, is given depth by the promise that "to everyone who conquers, I will give permission to eat from the tree of life that is in the paradise of God" (v. 7).

The complexity of the situation that has emerged between the stories of the tree of life and the Roman occupation of the late first century AD is large, and yet the image conjures a memory. Return to that first love, and the reward is a return to the Garden of Genesis.

The tree that gives life without ceasing is again promised. This isn't regression; instead, it is a coming around again. It is an image first brought to life in Genesis (Gen 2:9) and the promise to Adam and Eve, and through that first image we start to see how helpful this memory is—it is an image that all will be made right despite present evidence to the contrary.

When John's vision brings up this image, a tree of life with green leaves lolling in an imagined breeze, it taps into their memory of a story they heard as children. The story has changed, however, and now instead of passive recipients they are active protagonists longing for the tree that represents fulfillment, hope, and life to the full. Rome is now their Babylon, hacking the tree of life at the roots.

Imagine how a people who were facing death daily would receive the promise—that image of the tree—of eating and living eternally without interruption?

Of course, they could do what many of us do with our memories—declare them to be fairy tales of a long-forgotten youth. "We've heard that tree story before. We've progressed and moved on." Yet the story captivates us somehow.

Without the memory of the places we've been, those simple and early stories of hope and health, the present and future will make little sense. The first things, the first loves, are often the hardest to part with. It is important to see the grammar of John's poetry here; the statement about Ephesus's departure is not from some early, contemptible, sophomoric kind of love but from a first and greater love.

To remain true to our first love requires knowing what it means to stay true *here and now*, not just one day in the future. It is to remember our vows that shape our habits and thoughts around fidelity to our spouse. It means remembering provision even when the darkness of our fi-

> *To remain true to our first love requires knowing what it means to stay true here and now, not just one day in the future.*

nances prompts us to search for other ways of securing income. It means loving our headstrong teenager.

In these moments of in-between, we need a love that helps us live within the tension of contingency.

LOVE PREPARES US FOR CONTINGENCY

What often breaks our will to "be here now" is our discomfort with *contingency*, the idea of a present-tense "maybe." Many of us live here each day. This tension is palpable in many of the Bible's narratives, including the idea that God is the God of both the righteous and the unrighteous (Mt 5:45). It is the philosophical way of saying every experience and memory of this moment *matters*.

Philosophically, contingency is the "status of propositions that are neither true under every possible valuation nor false under every possible valuation."[6] In language the Ephesians would understand, contingency is living between Babylon's (Rome's) reign and Babylon's fall. It is the place where both good and evil, hope and despair, righteous and unrighteous sit across from each other, making unbroken eye contact.

Contingency is where we hear the echoes of our memories of love and faith, and ask, "Yeah, but what about *this* mess in front of us?"

Even when our focus is love, when we center all of our energies on the Great Commandment, it does not mean immediate resolution. John's message to the seven churches was immense, sweeping, and hopeful. However, not a single person lived to see the symbolism become full reality. They lived in the valley, but with the hope of light on the other side. We do the same, and in this valley we experience many of our most formative moments.

We may long for the promised tree of life, but we often experience emotional and personal consequences in the process.

I once saw a bumper sticker that said, "Are you sure you turned the oven off?" I immediately thought, *Wait, did I?* Curiosity led to panic, and I began to search through my working memory for confirmation.

Setting aside for the moment that I only use the oven in *rare* circumstances, I had to give thought to why this random message could cause me to search my memory for a flick of a wrist, a pressed button, and gas ceasing to flow into our house. Panic set in. *Maybe I didn't!*

I've since found a simple solution to this distraction.

Before I leave for a trip, I walk around the house and take pictures of our doors and appliances. I digitally document their off and locked positions. Often, when I'm at a stoplight or preparing for takeoff, I'll pull out my phone, look at the pictures, and breathe a sigh of relief.

Technology can be an adequate way to manage anxiety, apparently.

It is interesting that the *act* of taking these pictures doesn't create a fail-safe memory, but I can look at the pictures to re-member that things will be fine upon my return home. The house will be secure, standing, and safe. Then I can be *present* wherever my travels may lead.

The photos confirm my actions when there is no other way to assure myself. They, in a way, confirm Julian of Norwich's oft-repeated blessing, "All shall be well, and all shall be well, and all manner of thing shall be well."[7] Staring at the digital image of knobs on our stove, I whisper this blessing: "The stove shall be well. The house shall be well. All manner of neighborhood thing shall be well."

Of course, it does not mean when I return that the house won't be in ruins from some *other* unexpected disaster. A memory only captures what we have access to through our personal expe-rience and perspective. So our memories create a future in which we can anticipate most things, but not all.

In this contingency, I give my attention and loyalty to the pic-tures. They help me be here now. The issue in contingency is always, What am I going to give my attention and my allegiance to here and now?

LOVE AND ALLEGIANCE

When we adjust our minds and step into the world of the Ephesian Christians, we see people unemployed because of their faith. We see grandmothers who have only mental images of their faithful grandsons due to the stroke of Caesar's blade. We see husbands and wives giving thanks that another day has gone by and *they're both still here*. We begin to see the dynamic nature of Revelation.

To be committed to the story of life with Jesus in community with his people was to be an enemy of the state. It meant possible imprisonment, even death.

Compromise with the empire was to reject what gave them meaning and hope and to betray those in their community who kept to their belief that the world had only one true King, Jesus. It meant a death of a different kind.

Every decision we make carries the scent of this kind of commitment. When I give myself to something—to a game on my phone, to a conversation, to a travel commitment or a project—I am proclaiming my *allegiance*.

By default, that which we give our allegiance to is the thing we wish to become. The churches of Revelation craved Caesar's favor because it saved their lives, but it also put them on a path toward becoming just like him.

Of course, our present allegiance entails commitment based on the memories we have of being *faithful* or *committed* to Jesus. The Scripture, prayer, teaching, and community we have engaged in up to this point give us a story and a script for understanding the deep and transformational impact of King Jesus.

We, like the audience of Revelation, are formed to understand the King and his kingdom in a particular way.

Allegiance then is the response of our heart to what matters most. What matters most is formed by our scripts, which, as we know, arise from our stories built on memories. When we look at what we give our allegiance to, and we wish to shift the target toward Christ or toward a different expression of Christian faith, we are required to investigate our scripts and the memory-filled stories that support and sustain them.

These memories invoke our allegiance and ask, Who are we, and whose are we? Allegiance is the memory of first love—the one who brought us to the moment where we are.

Living in light of John's Revelation means we are in on the joke that the script has changed and the emperor is naked, as he has always been. The unmasking of the powers and principalities is satire of the richest kind (Col 2:15).

We, like the first audience of Revelation, can laugh at the posturing of the "powers" even when they breathe out threats because they simply do not get the joke. The cross is the grand joke God plays on the power structures of the world.

This is why John's vision starts with an introduction: "Do not be afraid; I am the first and the last, and the living one. I was dead, and see, I am alive forever and ever" (Rev 1:17-18).

Whatever the powers may tell you, whatever force they may exert, store this shell and let it flow into the script of your life. The great joke is that though death may be used as leverage, *remember* there is One who begs to differ. Let that memory become *action*.

When we look at what we give our allegiance to, and we wish to shift the target toward Christ or toward a different expression of Christian faith, we are required to investigate our scripts and the memory-filled stories that support and sustain them.

Which particular power we refer to here matters little, honestly. Formation is the process of reckoning with *all* competing powers. The power of our compulsions, the power of our relational or vocational worlds, and especially the power of our assumed stories are all vital playgrounds for our growth and development into who God made us to be.

TO CONQUER

John's promise to the Ephesians extends "to everyone who conquers" (Rev 2:7). While this is a yet-to-be reality, it is also a present-tense call. As we will soon see, a great deal of the language in Revelation is a reminder of a wondrous future, but none of it comes apart from a call to "be here now." Overcome where you are, when you are, how you are, and by what you are. This is the way forward through the contingencies of life.

In the midst of difficult circumstances, we reach for memories that tell us there is a reason to overcome. We tend to forget that truth in times of high anxiety and stress because our brains are wired to do that. Researchers say that anxiety and stress can cause excessive levels of cortisol, which can significantly affect memory.[8]

Our minds are constantly looking *forward* in contingent situations—*How do we get out of this?* But what if the saving grace is actually remembering stories that speak to our present pain?

Paul speaks of it this way:

Do not worry about anything, but in everything by prayer and supplication with thanksgiving let your requests be made known to God. And the peace of God, which surpasses all understanding, will guard your hearts and your minds in Christ Jesus.

Finally, beloved, whatever is true, whatever is honorable, whatever is just, whatever is pure, whatever is pleasing, whatever is commendable, if there is any excellence and if there is anything worthy of praise, think about these things. (Phil 4:6-8)

David Dark echoes this point eloquently: "If you want to make it back home you have to keep moving forward, consenting— again and again—to being transformed by the renewing of your mind, to learning, revisiting and resisting once more the bad habit of mistaking your sense of reality for reality itself."[9]

We remember things that are lovely and praiseworthy, we remind ourselves that our deeper life comes from the love of Jesus (both subjective and objective), and then we also realize that in the contingency there are some things that are too far off and too high for us to engage. We pray in the contingency remembering that there are things "too great and too marvelous for me" (Ps 131:1).

In fact, it appears that John's apocalypse is built to remind the churches of this.

NONEXISTENT CAVES

The imagery of Revelation itself testifies to this strange contingency. For example, in the midst of the visions, John writes: "The sky vanished like a scroll rolling itself up, and every mountain and island was removed from its place" (Rev 6:14). In our desire to see Revelation as a set of tumblers that when set in proper order will dispatch our fears, anxieties, and oppressors, we read this image as something that will *literally* happen. I remember looking up at the sky in my newfound faith and imagining the clouds slipping underneath each other as great unseen hands spun the fabric of the sky (as in Revelation 6).

The problem with seeing Revelation 6:14 as a literal meteorological event is, ironically, Revelation 6:15, which says,

Then the kings of the earth and the magnates and the generals and the rich and the powerful, and everyone, slave and free, hid in the caves and among the rocks of the mountains, calling to the mountains and rocks, "Fall on us and hide us from the face of the one seated on the throne and from the wrath of the Lamb; for the great day of their wrath has come, and who is able to stand?" (Rev 6:15-17)

Contingency is most definitely the life that occurs when the mountains are both removed from their places (v. 14) *and* are also available as a refuge to those who feared the loss of their own power (v. 15). Contingency is the spiritual notion of the great both-and. It is the crisis moment of "every memory belongs." The memories of God's care for us in the past help us to trust, to remain faithful, even when things are contingent, when they are unsettled and uncertain.

The great challenge will be to make sense of our faith in times of contingency. Barbara Brown Taylor outlines contingency best:

After so many years of trying to cobble together a way of thinking about God that makes sense so that I can safely settle down with it, it all turns to *nada*. There is no permanently safe place to settle. I will always be at sea, steering by stars. Yet as dark as this sounds, it provides great relief, because it now sounds truer than anything that came before.[10]

To allow contingency to form us, we have to embrace the in-between nature of life and actively remember the shells we have collected, shells through which God speaks clearly of his presence in the contingency. It is a moment when we wait. It is a moment when we cry. It is a moment of frustration.

There is perhaps a no better picture of contingency than the process of moving.

GO WEST, YOUNG ONES

As my family closed out a period of moving between homes once again, my wife and I noticed that over time our ability to gracefully withstand the contingency of moving has increased. Perhaps that is because our moving stories have been filled with challenge and trial.

For example, in late 2000 we moved cross-country from the gentle, rolling hills of central Ohio to the slate-level prairie of Illinois. Holley had flown out early to establish herself in her new job and was staying with her parents who lived in the community we were moving to. I was tasked with loading all of our possessions and one of our two cars onto the moving truck. Seemed simple enough at the time. If I had only known what shells I would collect on this journey.

A friend showed up, and we began loading furniture and boxes. The December air was wet and heavy, and the pavement already soaked by rain proved to be slicker by the moment as we loaded the truck. Apparently, the laws of physics can be horrific pranksters. For whatever reason, the weight of our few packed boxes caused the truck to shift, sliding on its tires into the grassy margins between our parking lot and a nearby fence.

Driving a heavy truck out of wet grass proved impossible—the immense tires simply spun on the grass and into the mud. We tried a variety of "good ideas" of how to get out of the mess before finally relenting.

I looked at my friend and said, "What are we going to do?"

He looked at me in disbelief. We had no prior experience with giant, mud-bound trucks to use as a gauge for this particular moment. No shells to examine.

We called a tow truck, which brought the moving truck back to the asphalt, and sometime around 1 a.m. we finally went to sleep, hoping to gain some momentum on the nearly six-hour drive the next day.

We woke to soaked streets. Everything was in the midst of a mild downpour. Arranging the last details soaked our clothes through, and by the time I managed the beast of a moving truck onto public roads I could feel the water *squishing* in my shoes.

A funny thing happened on the way to Illinois, however. Crossing the midline of Indiana, we noticed a temperature drop. Water beads on the windshield that an hour ago were quivering wet in the wind were now motionless—frozen.

The temperature was dropping rapidly, and the water coat of Ohio gradually but relentlessly turned into the icy shroud of Illinois. Inches of snow began to fall, which would not fully melt until March. The only thing I could do was drive and keep my eyes on the endpoint, the resolution, the denouement of this long and strange trip.

We arrived in Springfield, Illinois, still wet from our loading process earlier in the day and shivering with a chill that an aging rental-truck heater simply could not amend. I pulled the truck into a public parking area where I met my father-in-law, and the hope was to roll my car off the trailer and take only the truck to our new apartment.

The car sat on the trailer, encrusted with ice. When I attempted to put the key into the lock, I met resistance. The tip of the key went in, but no further. The Ohio rain had seeped into the door locks and froze solid somewhere near Danville, Illinois.

You have to be kidding me.

My father-in-law and I quickly found a solution. He drove home and came back with a small propane torch. In a scene fit for any number of situation comedies, I would sit in my father-in-law's car (windows open, because "safety first") and heat the key with the torch, then hop out and run to my car to repeatedly jam the key in the lock, breaking up the ice.

We repeated this process for what seemed like hours until we finally had success. We left the car and the moving truck in their places at the new apartment and returned to my in-laws'. My friend and I were soaked, then frozen, then frustrated, and now semi-thawed. We sat down to pizza and ate like men on death row. It was over. Finally.

Moving homes, jobs, relationships, or even movement along the stages of the spiritual journey is all about forming us to deal with contingency. Things are up in the air. When everything you own is in a box—*I think it's that one, over there*—you have introduced contingency into the world. Things may not fit in the future, things may need to be rearranged. This is the land in-between, where our memories help carry us through what we don't know. In our spiritual journey with Jesus, we may not have the same default response to fear and anxiety that we did before. Our defaults have changed. Our assumptions change.

We still carry our shells and their neuron-borne memories, and we still imagine the story written in stars above our heads. But the script? The script for our lives has now taken on new flavors and contours that we didn't expect.

We learn to live in the contingency, like the place between the honeymoon and a firm, flint-like marriage. We learn to live in the place between failure and faith beyond limitations. We learn to live into the seemingly devastating hunger of fasting for the future memory of a deep well of strength available to us somewhat by default.

We learn to be here now.

PAUSE

The book of Revelation is a majestic but exhausting read that takes a great deal of our attention and the faithful suspension of our disbelief.

This pause is built to allow us to reflect on a major theme from Revelation that impacts our memories. In this pause, we will focus on the concept of *contingency*.

First, find a place where you can control the noise around you. You may have to find a good-enough spot for now, or come back to this pause later.

As you remain in silence, knowing God is with you, let the idea of *contingency*—things sitting unfinished, the "divine maybe"—flow into your mind. Perhaps repeat the word out loud and let the letters and syllables flow slowly, meditating on the word as you speak it.

Allow yourself time to listen for what God may have to say to you about the concept of *contingency*, specifically whether there are tensions you need to balance that help you stay rooted even in the midst of *contingency*.

11

A FUTURE MEMORY

We are creatures with a mystery in our hearts that is bigger than ourselves.

JAMES BRYAN SMITH

Neurosurgeon Richard Restak uses a term that helps give clarity to the role of our memories in formation for the future. He calls it "future memory," or a vision of what *can* be based on what we've heard or seen in the past. As an example, he says that he frequently invites students into a hospital to show them some of the functions and activities that go along with being a neurosurgeon, an opportunity that might make them interested in neurosurgery.

He says,

They start medical school and residency, and then there are certain days when they think, *This isn't worth it, why did I ever get into this?* And the future memory is that part that revives, and they feel again what they experienced when they made up their minds about what they wanted to do. They don't just live in the moment, they know they're having a rough time, but they have their goal in mind and want to achieve it.[1]

We have future dreams, future expectations—to find a partner in life, to marry and raise kids, to do productive work, to be physically and emotionally healthier in a year than we are right now.

How does a place like Ephesus sustain their first love in their dire situation under the thumb of Rome? They cultivated a future memory, and John gave them the imaginative fuel to do so: "To everyone who conquers, I will give permission to eat from the tree of life that is in the paradise of God" (Rev 2:7).

> *Love catalyzes the vision of a future memory. Future memory gives everyone a reason to be resilient.*

Love catalyzes the vision of a future memory. Future memory gives everyone a reason to be resilient. The communities in Revelation had nothing but promises, images, and pictures. Underneath the images, however, a future memory is being born.

Three little blackbirds are tattooed on my wife's arm, images that tell the story of a future memory. They are images that remind us of future hope in present trials. We are called to remember that the future is going to be different. We remember a revelation of something that has yet to happen, but it is connected deeply to things that have already occurred.

We hear it echoed deeply in Revelation 21:1-4: "No more tears." Renowned Bible commentator Austin Farrer says in Revelation "we shall expect . . . 'a rebirth of images.'"[2]

The imagery in Revelation associated with Babylon speaks to this idea. The imagery of the great "whore" (Rev 17:4-5) being decimated invited the Ephesians to remember that *there was no such thing as Babylon at the time John was writing.* Babylon was a pervasive and potent force against God's people in much of the Old Testament, but in the first century AD, Babylon was no more.

Remember, nations like Babylon fall.

Remember, because it can happen again.

The future memory of Babylon falling—with Rome now playing the symbolic role of Babylon—gave strength and energy to the Ephesian Christians. It shaped their passions, thoughts, and actions to know that many great evils had come before and had fallen. The pain of the present has to be seen in the light of a future memory. Babylon has fallen before and it will fall once again. John's visions are calling the Mediterranean churches to cultivate the memory of a future that is yet to happen through the love of the One who brought them that far in the first place.

Daniel Amen says in *Stones of Remembrance*, "Memory enables us to bring the joys, dreams, and lessons of yesterday into today. As we recall God's faithfulness, we remain centered and growing, and we move forward with a sense of purpose."[3]

Give place, John says, to the love that sustains you through this kind of thing. Let the energy of a future memory pour into that love. It is the only way forward. We become the kind of people who examine our memories for the times when those who sought to kill us died their own death.

Past life crises now form us to see future crises in a more hopeful context.

LOVE CREATES RESILIENCE

Ephesus is living on a generator. The energy for life under Domitian is found when their first great love is made central once again. To find their way back requires memory, past experiences that tell stories and compose scripts of what life is meant to look like as we walk in the light of Jesus.

Revelation steps in to remind us that our memories dot the continuum between God's Alpha and Omega (Rev 1:8), and therefore he has been present and will be present throughout the tales our memories tell. On that continuum we are drawn to what matters most—love.

The message to the Ephesians and to us in our trials is a reminder: *Remember the thing that oriented you once and can settle you once again. Remember your first love, the Son of Man, and stand strong—remember the first love that makes you resilient.*

Everything that has gone before, when ordered and oriented around love for God, others, and self (Mt 22:37-40), is made richer and fuller. When we remember love, when we put our steps in order based on our memory of that which is worthy of love, we create an image of the future, "who is and who was and who is to come" (Rev 1:8).

In John's world there are some, the arrogant, who exploit and exterminate others because of an allegiance to the world's true king, Jesus. The way of Jesus threatens the soft blanket of comfort that power provides to those living in a world devoid of redemption and imagination. Grace is an intrusion into that world.

Those whose goal is domination have no resilience. Resilience is animated by love alone.

Resilience is found when we are willing to live in the love of Jesus even when life experiences threaten to overwrite our memories, stories, and scripts of that love.

The memory of Revelation is meant to *sustain*. Our experiences of hope and light keep us moving when darkness comes near. Revelation calls on our memories, stories, and scripts, redeeming them and building resilience on the foundation of the love that flows from "one like the Son of Man" (Rev 1:13). From there, we can move through broken shells and be shaped into the potent and beautiful beings we are in the living memory of God.

Sheryl Sandberg writes with honesty and grace after the tragic death of her husband. She says, "Resilience is the strength and speed of our response to adversity" and adds "and we can build it."[4] Resilience through love primes us for disappointment, unmet expectations, things not going the way our good creation was intended to go by the Alpha and Omega.

A hard-pressed family of Jesus-followers living in the Mediterranean needed the same. Strength and speed come from a foundation of memory—stories and scripts that give those of us living real lives a place to begin in times of adversity and oppression.

In truth, Revelation is the culmination of our entire understanding of memory from the Scriptures. Resilience comes through freedom, freedom from the false self and movement toward the liberation of remembering who we are meant to be. And resilience comes through failure. The calluses of wisdom form on our hearts and hands, and we stand in a place we have been before and embrace the lessons that have come in the interim.

Resilience comes in the encounter with the God of reality through our emotions. The songs of suffering, protection, provision, and confusion that enliven the psalms create experiences and memories of God's interaction with us even when our hearts grow unruly.

Then, in the stunning drama of Jesus, resilience is knowing that death is most certainly defeated, but also that formation in Christ creates a path we can follow in every circumstance.

Resilience is the fruit of memory. We remember that these things have come to pass before, and they will come again. Yet when they come, they are not exactly the same.

Resilience tells a new story for us but also for the world. John O'Donohue writes, "The life and passion of a person leave an imprint on the ether of a place. Love does not remain within the heart, it flows out to build secret tabernacles in a landscape."[5]

Cultivating resilience requires that we engage Revelation's memory and our own with one particular creative characteristic —*imagination*.

WE MUST PICTURE IT

It isn't an accident that John's apocalyptic writing pulls from images that would have been familiar to the persecuted ones in the Mediterranean: a Son of Man in blazing white, lions, lambs, horses, earthquakes, blood, solar and lunar chaos were all recognized images among those churches. The difference is that in the moment, those memories are combined in new and fresh ways to ignite the imagination of a weary, hunted tribe of Christians.

In other words, forming their imagination through their memories would also create the resilience they needed.

Thomas Merton echoes this idea, saying, "Imagination is the creative task of making symbols, joining things together in such a way that they throw new light on each other and on everything around them."[6]

Revelation uses memories to inspire imagination, the kind of imagination that takes a situation of death and depravity and finds a beautiful way forward within. The darker the night, the harder we have to imagine the light. The definition of faith is "the assurance of things hoped for, the conviction of things not seen. Indeed, by faith our ancestors received approval. By faith we understand that the worlds were prepared by the word of God, so that what is seen was made from things that are not visible" (Heb 11:1-3).

Imagining those unseen things in the midst of our daily duels or in the midst of Mediterranean massacres helps us develop the "future memory" that is so desperately needed. It is a faith rooted in ancestors remembered as the "cloud of witnesses" (Heb 12:1) because they all began with the imagination to see what had not yet been revealed.

In the words of Michael Gorman, the power of Revelation is that "it can transform the imagination with respect to how we perceive and live in relation to God, others, and the world."[7] In other words, John's message was strong enough to strengthen the heart and the hands, and impenetrable enough to inspire and enliven the head. This is the beauty of apocalyptic literature—it fires the imagination. Of course, our imagination must draw from a preexisting well in order to break new ground and picture things beyond our experience.

We need resilience to imagine John's picture of a being and a throne, which resembles a memory from Daniel that Babylon will fall (Dan 7:9-13; Rev 1:12-15). We need resilience to imagine twenty-four thrones, a memory of both the twelve tribes of Israel and the twelve disciples of Jesus, around the main throne (Rev 4:4).

Though the thrones and elders are images capturing the intense imagination of the persecuted church, the theme is clear: *cling to your resilience, because those who represent you are going to prevail, and the God who loves you will triumph over the empire.* Nevertheless, our resilience often wanes because we prefer the literal images and happenings coursing through the pages of Revelation.

Our great energies in reading Revelation instead have been used to inspect the divine administration of the end of all things. So it seems strange to envision Revelation as a work of imagination. Yet that is what the book is, and that is where the book intersects our own experience.

Our resilience in the present comes from memories that stoke our imagination for what the future may be, just ahead.

Our resilience in the present comes from memories that stoke our imagination for what the future may be, just ahead.

MY FUTURE MEMORY

A picture of my wife and me, taken in 2010 or 2011 while we were on vacation in Wisconsin brings a wide smile every time I see it. We had been married for at least ten years and were finally getting a sense of each other. As an aside, if you are walking the road of marriage and wondering if things will ever begin to take on that beautiful shape that you had always envisioned, please keep walking. Dig deep and fill the well of your relationship with grace and faith, look for the way of Jesus in the way of marriage, and know that *beautiful* does not mean "perfect." A future beauty is possible.

The picture tells a story of hard times gone by.

We had spent the previous five years walking through a challenging ministry season, my mother-in-law's liver transplant and subsequent health journey, a miscarriage and then a healthy pregnancy that led to my daughter's arrival. Our bodies and spirits sang with new health as we committed to eating differently and had both lost sixty pounds. I had run the Chicago

Marathon, pushing this newfound health to the highest point—
at least that I could imagine. We were serving in a new church,
but little did we know we were about to learn critical lessons
about our true selves.

I think back to this picture often. We are in the kitchen of our
rental condo, me embracing my wife, my pitiful one-day stubble
bearing no white whiskers as it does today. In one hand I'm
holding a spatula, having taken a break from flipping the morning
pancakes. We are both grinning as if we know something that no
one else knows. The past years had formed us in such a way that
we believed we had cheated the house, we had peeked at the an-
swers to the test, and though we would have difficult roads ahead
we knew we were moving toward a more beautiful country.

Formation through memory gives us this kind of gift. To stand
in that kitchen with a spatula in hand, knowing the glee of
flipping pancakes for my family in the morning and looking
forward to later resting in my special chair, I had a sense that we
could deal with the present should it change without warning. It
was a sense of being impervious, which I now know was delu-
sional. But when we are harnessed into a future hope, we often
believe the present will be easy and without difficulty. It was not
the case for Holley and me, and it certainly was not the case for
the churches of Revelation.

However, we have this picture, this moment in time that said,
"There is life that transcends and flows out of difficulty. Don't
forget it, but instead long for it now as it comes slowly in the future."

Pioneering neurologist Endel Tulving agrees, saying the self is
not limited to traveling backward (in memory); it can also journey
forward to the future. In Tulving's view, "The episodic memory

system (experiences plus facts) is as much about our projecting our imagination into the future as it is about reliving the past."[8]

I can look at this picture and whisper to myself, "Babylon fell before. It will fall again."

We need a mystical, explosive picture of *culmination* in the present for the future that is yet to come. It is the train of memories bearing down on our present oppression in a way that makes us resilient enough to face the pressures and pains than come our way.

It is the thought of home on a long drive.

It is the belief in health after a long illness or addiction.

It is the hope of redemption after tearful confession.

It is the longing for vocation at the end of a long season of education.

When I pray today, it is an act of culmination. The wisdom and grace that I have learned through the years, from praying in tears during difficult moments to dozing off mid-sentence in my early faith, all come together when I close my eyes in this present moment.

> *The God who loves is the God of memory, the one who builds resilience and prepares us for the unavoidable contingency of living in the here and now.*

We then commence praying for the present as we build toward the future.

I pray in the contingency as an act of resiliency.

When I serve others, when I create something that I pray will give light and life to those who will hear it or use it, I bring the cutting-room floor of my creative life with me. Every scrap or shard of phrase and insight comes forward into this moment, where it might possibly find its purpose.

I serve in the contingency as an act of resiliency.

To lose ourselves in the great and beautiful love of God is to be formed by the memories, stories, and scripts of care, provision, and vindication so we can long for the moments that have yet to arrive. To live in the land between, in contingency, is to embrace the suffering of the present salved by a memory of a future that is yet to come.

That is what it means to remember in Revelation.

It is what it means to embrace our memories, stories, and scripts today.

The God who loves is the God of memory, the one who builds resilience and prepares us for the unavoidable contingency of living in the here and now.

Remember the three little birds.

PAUSE

As a follow up to the pause in chapter 10, this pause is built to allow us to reflect on a the other major concept in Revelation that impacts our memories. In this pause, we will focus on the concept of *resilience*.

Again, find a place where you can control the noise around you. You may have to find a good-enough spot for now, or come back to this pause later.

As you remain in silence, knowing God is with you, let the idea of *resilience*—developing a "future memory" that gives strength to our redeemed stories and scripts—flow into your mind. As with *contingency*, repeat the word *resilience* out loud and let the letters and syllables flow slowly, meditating on the word as you speak it.

Allow yourself time to listen for what God may have to say to you about the concept of *resilience*, specifically whether there is a future memory that God is weaving together for you to give you hope and energy for the future.

12

A CLOSING POST-IT NOTE

We shall not cease from exploration
And the end of all our exploring
Will be to arrive where we started,
And know the place for the first time.

T. S. ELIOT

We have stories to tell to the world, stories that swell within the shells we have collected.

The fruit of our memories is that there is something of value in the path that stretches behind us. Redeeming our memories and living out a new script in the present is the most precious thing we can pass on.

It is the wisdom of the true self in motion that Moses both came to and gave away just beyond the Jordan. It is the emotional life David and the psalmists presented on their dive into the human soul. It is the taken, blessed, and broken reality exemplified in Jesus and put on display through our invitation to lean into the new story that he envisions for us.

It is, however, much more than that.

There is no greater news than a human being living out the script of transformation while collecting both broken and beautiful shells. Formation and discipleship *are* good news, and often we in the church bury the lede by separating the life of apprenticeship to Jesus from evangelism.

That being said, there is one last shell remaining from Jesus' Eucharistic image: "After blessing it he broke it, [and] *gave* it to them" (Mk 14:22).

Many of our memories, stories, and scripts affect our part of the spinning globe because they have been given to us. Thinking of these elements of our past—being chosen, blessed, and even being broken—as gifts from a compassionate Christ reshapes them.

Joyce Rupp sees this idea through the metaphor of a dependable but worn teacup. "I have learned that I have flaws, chips, and stains, just as any well-used cup may have, but that these markings of a well-traveled life need not prevent me from being a valuable gift for others."[1]

> *Redeeming our memories and living out a new script in the present is the most precious thing we can pass on.*

We are given stories of being shaped to live in freedom from addiction, debt, and self-destruction.

We are given stories of provision in which the very thing we need inexplicably comes in time.

Or we engage with God in our memories, and he *gives back* some of our most broken shells—experiences of pain from which we bear emotional or even physical marks, and though the shell is still rough to the touch we see the band of color within.

They are not only gifts for us but for the world. The suffering of self, the absence of God, the learnings from the failure of the false self, and the wisdom of the wilderness match corresponding gaps in the stories and scripts of our families, friends, and neighbors.

Is it possible that the best news we can offer is to reveal a person formed by Jesus through all of our memories, as if every memory belongs?

Henri Nouwen once again paints a beautiful picture of this *given* reality: "As the Beloved ones, our greatest fulfillment lies in becoming bread for the world. That is the most intimate expression of our deepest desire to give ourselves to each other."[2]

It is only in breaking bread—the same chosen and blessed bread we identify with—that there is enough to feed the world. The mystery in this is, of course, that every memory belongs, including our memories of being torn, and finding in Jesus a sense of the reality of being a person in flesh.

The resolution or the redemption of the bittersweet parts of our memories comes when we take that which is difficult and disparate in our scripts and engage it with Jesus to make that bittersweetness a beautiful gift. Then we may give a gift to other loved ones who feel abandoned, graceless, and deformed. But what might this look like as we live it?

We possess our memories in order that, redeemed and re-envisioned, they may become stories that merit telling.

REMEMBERING A WORK ON REMEMBERING

This book was written in four different homes, including one generously opened to me by others and two that I paid a mortgage on in the same calendar year. This book was also written while serving in two different congregations. At one point I remember feeling that the book had gotten away from me—when I came back to the blinking cursor, it felt as if I was walking in undiscovered country. The rush, transition, and stress caused my memory and focus to drift.

And now I close the album that contains the snapshots of that year.

I will remember this season as a time when God invited me to come to the table, a time when I had to trust within the contingency and hope with resiliency.

I will remember the process of gaining wisdom about writing in transition, about embracing difficulty and finding joy.

I will remember the stripping away of the false self that continues to fall away like spiral wood shavings from a carpenter's tool.

I will feel the songs of my memory, the emotions of experience that come when walking the face of this world with God, feeling the ups and the downs.

My invitation for all of us is to regard our memories as gifts—moments of consideration and grace that we may grow into the memory bearers that God has fashioned us to be.

And may we know that the God who lives in *kairos* time—time outside of time—lives in our past, inspires our present, and enables our future. If we are but willing to recall.

ACKNOWLEDGMENTS

*I*t is no small task to write a book. However, there are some seasons that are more challenging than others. The book you hold in your hand was born in such a season—more of a winter, icy and firm, than a spring. In a season like this, I needed the people around me to help carry the book (and myself) to completion.

Without my wife, Holley, and daughter, Bailey, this book would not exist. They are both part of the story (and stories) I am privileged to tell. They also give up time so I can go to the office, close the blinds, and attempt to find "the flow."

Thanks to Mom and Dad Bente, Dad and Mom Tygrett, and Sis (Hillary Gore) for giving me memories that have served for my growth, encouragement, and redemption.

Sincere gratitude goes to the entire team at InterVarsity Press: Jeff Crosby, Cindy Bunch, Katelyn Beaty, Lori Neff, Alisse Wissman, and Krista Clayton for encouragement and partnership in the writing and publishing process.

Thanks to Don Gates of the Gates Group for his friendship and representation through the process of bringing a book like this to life.

Many thanks go to Josh Peigh and the team at Heartland Community Church for their graciousness during the initial stages of writing this book. Thanks to Jared Cacciatore and Kayla Acton, specifically for their interest and encouragement in the process.

Thanks to my family at Parkview Christian Church, specifically Tim Harlow, Bill Brown, Laurie Kamp, Dan Leverence, and Wayne Krahn for welcoming me back to Parkview with open arms.

Thanks also go to James Bryan Smith, James Catford, Kara Yuza, and the team at the Apprentice Institute for inviting me into the fold and onto the Apprentice Institute board. Thanks also to John Robinson and the folks at ACOM (Australia) for dialogues and encouragement that I am blessed to receive.

Thanks to everyone who subscribes to my blog at CaseyTygrett .com and to all who listen and subscribe to the otherWISE podcast, where ideas like this first see the light of day.

If I have forgotten you, it is because my semantic memory is overloaded with cortisol from the anxiety of finishing this project. If you read the book, you know what I mean.

Peace friends.

NOTES

INTRODUCTION: A QUESTION BEFORE REMEMBERING

[1]V. S. Ramachandran, *The Tell-Tale Brain: A Neuroscientist's Quest for What Makes Us Human* (New York: W. W. Norton, 2012), 4.

[2]*The Matrix*, directed by Lana Wachowski and Lilly Wachowski (Burbank, CA: Warner Bros., 1999).

1 HOW WE GOT HERE

[1]Susan Greenfield, *Mind Change: How Digital Technologies Are Leaving Their Marks on Our Brains* (New York: Random House, 2015), 203.

[2]Eric Kandel, *In Search of Memory: The Emergence of a New Science of Mind* (New York: W. W. Norton, 2017), 10.

[3]Dallas Willard, *Renovation of the Heart: Putting on the Character of Christ* (Colorado Springs: NavPress, 2002), 199.

[4]Joyce Rupp, *The Cup of Our Life: A Guide to Spiritual Growth* (Notre Dame, IN: Ave Maria Press, 2012), 28.

2 THE ART OF NOTICING SHELLS

[1]Kenneth L. Higbee, *Your Memory: How It Works and How to Improve It*, 2nd ed. (Boston: Da Capo Lifelong Books, 2008), 19.

[2]Edwin T. Morris, quoted in Diane Ackerman, *A Natural History of the Senses* (New York: Random House, 1991), 11.

[3]Joseph Jebelli, *In Pursuit of Memory: The Fight Against Alzheimer's* (New York: Little, Brown, 2017), 191.

[4]Joshua Foer, *Moonwalking with Einstein: The Art and Science of Remembering Everything* (New York: Penguin, 2011), 84.

[5]Petina Gappah, *The Book of Memory* (New York: Farrar, Straus, and Giroux, 2016), 14.

[6]Elizabeth Johnston and Leah Olson, *The Feeling Brain: The Biology and Psychology of Emotions* (New York: W. W. Norton, 2015), 183.

[7]David Eagleman, *Incognito: The Secret Lives of the Brain* (New York: Vintage Books, 2012), 21.

[8]James Elkins, quoted in Leighton Ford, *The Attentive Life: Discovering God's Presence in All Things* (Downers Grove: InterVarsity Press, 2008), 42.

⁹Foer, *Moonwalking with Einstein*, 33.

¹⁰Higbee, *Your Memory: How It Works*, 23.

¹¹Glenn Paauw, *Saving the Bible from Ourselves: Learning to Read and Live the Bible Well* (Downers Grove, IL: InterVarsity Press, 2016), 51-74.

¹²Sharon Begley, quoted in Susan Greenfield, *Mind Change: How Digital Technologies Are Leaving Their Marks on Our Brains* (New York: Random House, 2015), 62.

¹³"Pneumaplasticity?" Capuchin Franciscan Province of St. Joseph, accessed May 13, 2018, www.thecapuchins.org/news/documents/Homily010911.pdf.

3 LIVING WITH SHELLS

¹Lee Eisenberg, *The Point Is: Making Sense of Birth, Death, and Everything in Between* (New York: Hachette/Twelve, 2016), 33.

²James Bryan Smith, *The Magnificent Story: Uncovering a Gospel of Beauty, Goodness, and Truth* (Downers Grove, IL: InterVarsity Press, 2017), 5.

³This idea comes from Keith Anderson's book *A Spirituality of Listening: Living What We Hear* (Downers Grove, IL: InterVarsity Press, 2015. The Latin phrase is often used by composers and stage producers to talk about either a melody line or a subject theme that runs throughout an entire composition or production.

⁴See Richard C. Francis, *Epigenetics: The Ultimate Mystery of Inheritance* (New York: W. W. Norton, 2011).

⁵Elizabeth Rosner, *Survivor Café: The Legacy of Trauma and the Labyrinth of Memory* (Berkeley, CA: Counterpoint, 2017), 6-7.

⁶Rosner, *Survivor Café*, 4.

⁷Barbara Brown Taylor, *Learning to Walk in the Dark* (New York: HarperCollins, 2014), 126.

⁸Mike Yaconelli, *Messy Spirituality: God's Annoying Love for Imperfect People* (Grand Rapids: Zondervan, 2002), 69.

4 THE WEIGHT OF SHELLS

¹Frank Laubach, "Opening Windows to God," *Devotional Classics: Selected Readings for Individuals and Groups*, ed. Richard J. Foster and James Bryan Smith (New York: HarperCollins, 1993), 121.

²Margaret Bendroth, *A Spiritual Practice of Remembering* (Grand Rapids: Eerdmans, 2013), 11.

³Jean-Pierre de Caussade, "The Present Moment," in Foster and Smith, *Devotional Classics*, 231-32.

[4]Henri Nouwen, *The Inner Voice of Love: A Journey Through Anguish to Freedom* (New York: Image Books, 1999), 38.

[5]I have heard Jim use this phrase on several different occasions, both in speaking contexts and personal conversation.

[6]Jim Collins, "Five Stages of Decline," JimCollins.com, accessed October 5, 2018, www.jimcollins.com/concepts/five-stages-of-decline.html.

[7]William L. Holladay, "hoseb," *A Concise Hebrew and Aramaic Lexicon of the Old Testament* (Bellingham, WA: Logos Bible Software, 2000).

[8]David Seamands, *Healing Of Memories* (Wheaton, IL: Victor Books, 1985), 72.

[9]Elizabeth Rosner, *Survivor Café: The Legacy of Trauma and the Labyrinth of Memory* (New York: Counterpoint, 2017), xvi.

[10]Robert Madigan, *How Memory Works—And How to Make It Work For You* (New York: Guilford Press, 2015), 18.

[11]Bessel van der Kolk, *The Body Keeps the Score: Brain, Mind, and Body in the Healing of Trauma* (New York: Penguin, 2014), 180.

[12]van der Kolk, *Body Keeps the Score*, 181.

[13]Robert Mulholland, *The Deeper Journey: The Spiritual Journey of Discovering Your True Self* (Downers Grove, IL: InterVarsity Press, 2016), 85.

5 EVERY MEMORY BELONGS

[1]Richard Rohr, *Falling Upward: A Spirituality for the Two Halves of Life* (San Francisco: Jossey-Bass, 2011), xxxi.

[2]Rohr, *Falling Upward*, 8-9.

[3]Henri J. M. Nouwen, *The Wounded Healer: Ministry in Contemporary Society* (New York: Doubleday, 1979).

6 REMEMBERING WHO WE ARE

[1]Lee Eisenberg, *The Point Is: Making Sense of Birth, Death, and Everything in Between* (New York: Hachette/Twelve, 2016), 45.

[2]Joseph Hallinan, *Kidding Ourselves: The Hidden Power of Self-Deception* (New York: Crown, 2014), 2.

[3]Brené Brown, "Strong Back, Soft Front, Wild Heart," *On Being with Krista Tippett* (podcast). https://onbeing.org/programs/brene-brown-strong-back-soft-front-wild-heart-feb2018.

[4]Robert Mulholland, *The Deeper Journey. The Spiritual Journey of Discovering Your True Self* (Downers Grove, IL: InterVarsity Press, 2016), 27.

[5]Sue Monk Kidd, *When the Heart Waits: Spiritual Direction for Life's Sacred Questions* (San Francisco: HarperOne, 1990), 52.

[6]Parker Palmer, *Let Your Life Speak: Listening for the Voice of Vocation* (San Francisco: Jossey-Bass, 2000), 10.

[7]Ruth Haley Barton, *Strengthening the Soul of Your Leadership: Seeking God in the Crucible of Ministry* (Downers Grove, IL: InterVarsity Press, 2008), 73.

[8]Heather Kopp, *Sober Mercies: How Love Caught Up with a Christian Drunk* (New York: Jericho Books, 2013), 69.

[9]Frederick Buechner, *Wishful Thinking: A Seeker's ABC* (New York: HarperOne, 1993), 118-19.

[10]Mark Buchanan, *The Rest of God: Restoring Your Soul by Restoring Sabbath* (Nashville: Thomas Nelson, 2006), 87.

7 COMING BACK AGAIN

[1]*Memento*, directed by Christopher Nolan (Los Angeles: Newmarket Films, 2000).

[2]Glenn Paauw, *Saving the Bible from Ourselves: Learning to Read and Live the Bible Well* (Downers Grove, IL: InterVarsity Press, 2016), 99-100.

[3]Leighton Ford, *The Attentive Life: Discovering God's Presence in All Things* (Downers Grove, IL: InterVarsity Press, 2014), 36.

[4]Dick Swaab, *We Are Our Brains: A Neurobiography of the Brain, from the Womb to Alzheimer's* (New York: Penguin Books, 2014), 259.

[5]I have heard J. K. mention this in both public presentations and personal conversations. I recommend his book J. K. Jones, *What the Monks Can Teach Us* (Joplin, MO: College Press, 2004) for further reading.

[6]Eric R. Kandel, *In Search of Memory: The Emergence of a New Science of Mind* (New York: W. W. Norton, 2007), 10.

[7]Dallas Willard, quoted by James Bryan Smith in "Casey and James Bryan Smith Talk the Amazing True Story of God," *otherWISE*, June 11, 2018, www.caseytygrett .com/podcast/2018/6/8/episode-005-casey-and-james-bryan-smith-talk-about -a-vision-for-life.

[8]A good resource on the Enneagram is Ian Morgan Cron and Suzanne Stabile, *The Road Back to You* (Downers Grove, IL: InterVarsity Press, 2016).

[9]Mariano Sigman, *The Secret Life of the Mind: How Your Brain Thinks, Feels, and Decides* (New York: Little, Brown, 2017), 49.

[10]Thomas Merton, *What Is Contemplation?* (Springfield, IL: Templegate, 1978), 8.

[11]For the original framework I experienced, see "Kingdom Practice: Prayer of

Examen," *The Practice*, May 5, 2014, www.practicetribe.com/kingdom-practice
-prayer-of-examen.

[12]See Louis J. Puhl, ed., *The Spiritual Exercises of St. Ignatius: Based on Studies in the Language of the Autograph* (Chicago: Loyola Press, 1951).

8 I'VE FELT LIKE THIS BEFORE

[1]Janna Leyde, *He Never Liked Cake* (Bloomington, IN: Balboa Press, 2013), 68.

[2]Lisa Feldman Barrett, *How Emotions Are Made: The Secret Life of the Brain* (New York: Mariner Books, 2017), 31.

[3]Don Saliers and Emily Saliers, in Diana Butler Bass, *A People's History of Christianity: The Other Side of the Story* (New York: HarperOne, 2009), 170.

[4]Jonathan Cott, *On the Sea of Memory* (New York: Random House, 2005), 144.

[5]Elizabeth Johnston and Leah Olson, *The Feeling Brain: The Biology and Psychology of Emotions* (New York: W. W. Norton, 2015), xi.

[6]David Seamands, *Healing of Memories* (Wheaton, IL: Victor Books, 1985), 96-97.

[7]Dan B. Allender and Tremper Longman III, *Cry of the Soul: How Our Emotions Reveal Our Deepest Questions About God* (Colorado Springs: NavPress, 1994), 20, 24-25.

[8]Frederick Buechner, *Telling the Truth: The Gospel as Tragedy, Comedy, and Fairy Tale* (San Francisco: HarperSanFrancisco, 1977), 39.

[9]Francis Brown, Samuel Rolles Driver, and Charles Augustus Briggs, "*hebel*," in *Enhanced Brown-Driver-Briggs Hebrew and English Lexicon* (Oxford: Clarendon Press, 1906), Logos Bible Software.

[10]Barrett, *How Emotions Are Made*, 180.

[11]Bessel van der Kolk, *The Body Keeps the Score: Brain, Mind, and Body in the Healing of Trauma* (New York: Penguin, 2014), 176.

9 A FAMILIAR TABLE

[1]Rich Mullins, "The Love of God," *Rich Mullins: Songs 2*, Reunion Records, 1999.

[2]Andrew Peterson, "Dancing in the Minefields," *Counting Stars*, Centricity Music, 2010.

[3]Christine Pohl, *Making Room: Recovering Hospitality as a Christian Tradition* (Grand Rapids: Eerdmans, 1999), 39.

[4]Henri Nouwen, *Life of the Beloved: Spiritual Living in a Secular World* (New York: Crossroad, 1992).

[5]Nouwen, *Life of the Beloved*, 47.

[6]Lesslie Newbigin, quoted in Leighton Ford, *The Attentive Life: Discovering God's Presence in All Things* (Downers Grove, IL: InterVarsity Press, 2014), 91.

[7]Emilie Griffin, *Souls in Full Sail: A Christian Spirituality for Later Years* (Downers Grove, IL: InterVarsity Press, 2011), 89.

[8]Nouwen, *Life of the Beloved*, 56-57.

[9]Joshua Foer, *Moonwalking with Einstein: The Art and Science of Remembering Everything* (New York: Penguin, 2011), 203.

[10]Nouwen, *Life of the Beloved*, 71-72.

[11]Richard Rohr, *Falling Upward: A Spirituality for the Two Halves of Life* (San Francisco: Jossey-Bass, 2011), Kindle, loc 407.

10 REMEMBER, BE HERE NOW

[1]Larry Rasmussen, quoted in Diana Butler Bass, *A People's History of Christianity: The Other Side of the Story* (New York: HarperOne, 2009), 90.

[2]Eugene Peterson, *Reversed Thunder: The Revelation of John and the Praying Imagination* (New York: HarperCollins, 1988), 5.

[3]N. T. Wright, *Paul and the Faithfulness of God* (Minneapolis: Fortress Press, 2013), 340-41

[4]G. B. Caird, *The Revelation of Saint John*, Black's New Testament Commentary (Peabody, MA: Hendrickson, 1993), 3.

[5]Michael Gorman, *Reading Revelation Responsibly: Uncivil Worship and Witness, Following the Lamb into the New Creation* (Eugene, OR: Cascade Books, 2011), xv.

[6]"Contingency (philosophy)," Wikipedia, accessed July 25, 2018, https://en.wikipedia.org/wiki/Contingency_(philosophy).

[7]"Julian of Norwich," *Goodreads*, accessed October 1, 2018, www.goodreads.com/author/quotes/156980.Julian_of_Norwich.

[8]"How Anxiety Can Cause Memory Loss," CalmClinic, accessed May 14, 2018, www.calmclinic.com/anxiety/symptoms/memory-problems.

[9]David Dark, *Life's Too Short to Pretend You're Not Religious* (Downers Grove, IL: InterVarsity Press, 2016), 90.

[10]Barbara Brown Taylor, *Learning to Walk in the Dark* (New York: HarperCollins, 2014), 140.

11 A FUTURE MEMORY

[1]Richard Restak, quoted in Jonathan Cott, *On the Sea of Memory* (New York: Random House, 2005), 90.

[2]Austin Farrer, quoted in G. B. Caird, *The Revelation of Saint John*, Black's New Testament Commentary (Peabody, MA: Hendrickson, 1993), 11.

[3]Daniel Amen, *Stones of Remembrance: Healing Scriptures for Your Mind, Body, and Soul* (Carol Stream, IL: Tyndale House, 2017), xiii.

[4]Sheryl Sandberg, *Option B: Facing Adversity, Building Resilience, and Finding Joy* (New York: Alfred A. Knopf, 2017), 10.

[5]John O'Donohue, *Anam Cara: A Book of Celtic Wisdom* (New York: Harper-Collins, 1997), 19.

[6]Thomas Merton, in Esther De Waal, *The Celtic Way of Prayer: The Recovery of the Religious Imagination* (New York: Doubleday, 1997), xiv.

[7]Michael Gorman, *Reading Revelation Responsibly: Uncivil Worship and Witness, Following the Lamb into the New Creation* (Eugene, OR: Cascade Books, 2011), 8.

[8]Robert Madigan, *How Memory Works—And How to Make It Work for You* (New York: Guilford Press, 2015), 14.

12 A CLOSING POST-IT NOTE

[1]Joyce Rupp, *The Cup of Our Life: A Guide to Spiritual Growth* (Notre Dame, IN: Ave Maria Press, 2012), 12.

[2]Henri Nouwen, *Life of the Beloved: Spiritual Living in a Secular World* (New York: Crossroad, 1997), 89.

CONTACT
CASEY TYGRETT

*T*o connect with Casey, inquire about speaking engagements, check out his blog, or listen to the *Restlessness Is a Gift* podcast, go to caseytygrett.com.

Facebook: facebook.com/cktygrettauthor
Twitter: @cktygrett
Instagram: @cktygrett